KU-125-406

CONTENTS

v

CHAPTER IV

CHAPTER V

CHAPTER VI

HAIL AND FAREWELL

THE PASSING OF KING GEORGE V

A

HIS MAJESTY KING GEORGE V.

HAIL AND FAREWELL

THE PASSING OF KING GEORGE V

1865 1936

LONDON
THE TIMES PUBLISHING COMPANY LIMITED
PRINTING HOUSE SQUARE
1936

KING ALFRED'S COLLEGE
WINCHESTER

942.083
TIM

79638

MADE AND PRINTED IN GREAT BRITAIN

PREFACE

THIS book is published in response to widespread public demands for a record in permanent form of the sadly historic twelve days, January 17 to January 28, 1936—the period which opened with the first announcement of the illness of King George V and closed with the burial of his body in St. George's Chapel, Windsor. Based upon the record of events which appeared day by day in *The Times*, it tells in word and picture the complete story of the passing of King George and of the Empire's farewell. The narrative is interspersed with the leading articles in which expression was given to the public sense of loss. The penultimate chapter contains a symposium of tributes to King George as man and monarch, and the volume closes with a condensed version of the long biography which appeared in *The Times* on the morrow of his death.

CHAPTER I

THE LAST PHASE

IN accordance with his practice of spending the Christmas holidays with his family, King George, accompanied by Queen Mary, left Buckingham Palace on December 21, 1935, for Sandringham. There had been days of stress in international relations which had engaged His Majesty closely in deliberations with his Ministers ; and, to be out of the pressure of affairs for a brief while, it was with some such feeling as the sailor home from the sea that he made the journey, no soul foreseeing it was to be the last. He was a home-loving man, never happier than when his children and grandchildren were gathered round him. The party for Christmas included the present King, the Duke and Duchess of Gloucester, the Duke and Duchess of Kent, and Princess Elizabeth and Princess Margaret. Unfortunately, the Duke and Duchess of York were unable to join the gathering, the Duchess being ill at the time with influenzal pneumonia.

The invention of the radio has made real the aspiration of the " Great Family " (a phrase used by King George when speaking to his people a year before) ; and ever mindful of others the King, on the afternoon of Christmas Day, broke from his family circle for a short space to deliver a message to the millions of his subjects in the Empire. A few weeks later the radio was to be the medium of sorrowful tidings. It was the King's fourth Christmas broadcast. No one who listened to that resonant, kindly voice, heard that soft catch of emotion betrayed by His Majesty when expressing gratitude for the spontaneous offering of loyalty and affection called forth on his Silver Jubilee but a few months back, and was thrilled by the touch of whimsical modesty in the reference to the man who, " may God help him, has been placed upon the throne," could know he would hear

I

B

that voice no more. Though the dire proofs be all about us of the many misprisions of science, man not learning yet how to keep pace in use with the wonders his devising mind contrives, yet we can rejoice that there is one invention at least which in the reign of King George V became so well controlled and so finely adapted to the better part of human nature that it can be safely numbered as a blessing of civilization. The brotherhood of man is a far-off dream, but it is nearer reality than on the day of Burns's prayer : for on four successive Christmas Days the British family have held a world-wide reunion by tuning their wireless sets to listen to their great chief broadcasting his greetings to them. The accents of the last message still linger on the ear, but this history demands that King George's final public utterance should be given in full. His Majesty said :

I wish you all, my dear friends, a happy Christmas. I have been deeply touched by the greetings which in the last few minutes have reached me from all parts of the Empire. Let me in response send to each of you a greeting from myself. My words will be very simple but spoken from the heart on this family festival of Christmas.

The year that is passing—the twenty-fifth since my Accession—has been to me most memorable. It called forth a spontaneous offering of loyalty—and may I say of love—which the Queen and I can never forget. How could I fail to note in all the rejoicing not merely respect for the Throne, but a warm and generous remembrance of the man himself who, may God help him, has been placed upon it.

It is this personal link between me and my people which I value more than I can say. It binds us together in all our common joys and sorrows, as when this year you showed your happiness in the marriage of my son, and your sympathy in the death of my beloved sister. I feel this link now as I speak to you. For I am thinking not so much of the Empire itself as of the individual men, women, and children who live within it, whether they are dwelling here at home or in some distant outpost of the Empire.

In Europe and many parts of the world anxieties surround us. It is good to think that our own family of peoples is at peace in itself and united in one desire to be at peace with other nations—the friend of all, the enemy of none. May the spirit of good will and mutual helpfulness grow and spread. Then it will bring not only the blessing of peace but a solution of the economic troubles which still beset us.

2

To those who are suffering or in distress, whether in this country or in any part of the Empire, I offer my deepest sympathy. But I would also give a Christmas message of hope and cheer. United by the bonds of willing service, let us prove ourselves both strong to endure and resolute to overcome.

Once again as I close I send to you all, and not the least to the children who may be listening to me, my truest Christmas wishes, and those of my dear wife, my children, and grandchildren who are with me to-day. I add a heartfelt prayer that, wherever you are, God may bless and keep you always.

The address was a noble climax to a notable broadcasting programme, which in retrospect can be seen as part of a sad memoir. As a prelude to the message, the voices of children, some travelling 12,000 miles from New Zealand, joined in the message from the Empire : " God bless and keep his gracious Majesty the King."

A crowded year, in which the burden of anxieties abroad had mingled with the strain of joyful emotion over events at home, necessitated a quiet holiday at Sandringham. The King's custom was to do a great deal of shooting during the New Year visit, but on this occasion the shooting parties were led by the Duke of Kent. The King, however, accompanied some of the parties, riding his white pony. He went to the parish church each Sunday with members of the Royal Family, walking from Sandringham House, about a quarter of a mile through the gardens ; and had enjoyed a number of films shown at the House by their Majesties' special desire.

In these simple pleasures, which were dearest to the man in the monarch, the few tranquil days passed till the blow fell and the term was closed. There was still the ever-haunting loom of significant yet uncertain tasks to come, from which his troubled reign had given him but rare releases : one sign of fretful things ahead was the visit paid to Sandringham by Mr. Eden, newly created Secretary of State for Foreign Affairs, on the eve of his departure for Geneva. But there was no prevision in the public mind to check its hopes for the continued guidance of a wise counsellor till late on the afternoon of Friday, January 17, the evening newspapers announced that the King was confined to his room with a cold and that Lord Dawson of Penn and Sir Stanley Hewett had travelled to Sandringham. To the people at large the B.B.C. broadcast the news at half-past six. Late that

3

night came the first bulletin from Sandringham, with its ominous words " some disquiet."

It was in the following terms :

> The bronchial catarrh from which His Majesty the King is suffering is not severe, but there have appeared signs of cardiac weakness which must be regarded with some disquiet.
>
> FREDERIC WILLANS.
> STANLEY HEWETT.
> DAWSON OF PENN.

The bulletin was broadcast just before midnight. At once all dance music was faded out, while in every home in the kingdom, eyes looked up in sad surmise. To understand why " disquiet " among the doctors should at once arouse grave fears among the public, it is necessary to recall certain happenings of last year and also King George's severe illness in 1928. On the morning of January 18, when the above bulletin was published in the newspapers, a special correspondent of *The Times* was able to report that the King had slept peacefully ; but that reassurance was helpful only in the knowledge it conveyed that His Majesty was not suffering unduly. Last June, after the fatigue of the Jubilee celebrations, the King went to Sandringham to recuperate, and during his stay it was learned that he was suffering from an attack of bronchial catarrh and had been ordered two weeks' rest. A slight chill the same month prevented his attendance at the London County Council reception at the County Hall. For seven years King George's subjects had realized the increased necessity of safeguarding his health, and his occasional postponement of certain public engagements, though causing natural disappointment, was accepted as a proper precaution against taking risks in our changeable climate. That the public instinct was right in regarding the bulletin of January 17 with some feelings of dismay is borne out by the considered statement made by the Medical Correspondent of *The Times* on the morning of Monday, January 20 ; and it will aid the interpretation of events to break here the chronology of the bulletins and print that statement entire. It was as follows :

While the King's present illness is in no sense a recrudescence of the illness from which he suffered seven years ago, the anxieties which now

4

necessarily beset his doctors cannot be understood unless that severe and prolonged ordeal is borne in mind. Seven years ago the King's blood was actually invaded by a microbe which produced the condition known as septicaemia. Septicaemia is a much graver complaint than pneumonia ; it is always dangerous, and it is usually fatal.

It is striking testimony, therefore, to the recuperative power possessed by the patient that, in highly skilled hands, he made a complete recovery from his illness. But recovery, necessarily, was paid for by a heavy overdraft upon the powers of recuperation. The King was well again ; but he had expended strength which in the nature of things could not easily be regained.

In the seven years which have since elapsed His Majesty has given to his people a strenuous, a constant, and an indispensable service. That service has not, in fact, lacked its benefits to the King himself ; the revelation of loyalty and love, for example, which the Jubilee Celebrations afforded cannot but have exerted an exhilarating and tonic effect upon mind and body and thus have helped to restore the balance of strength. The King's doctors, moreover, by their constant watch over him, protected him from fatigue—as is proved by the evident enjoyment with which he performed all his public duties. Once or twice during the Jubilee Celebrations, as may be inferred, signs of fatigue must have been observed—for example, during Ascot Week, when he did not attend the races.

The King's present illness has occurred coincidently with the presence of influenza throughout the country, and this constitutes without doubt an added anxiety for his doctors. It has occurred, too, in mid-winter, when respiratory disease is always prevalent. The weather at Sandringham has not been favourable ; nor must it be forgotten that by the death of his sister a short time ago His Majesty suffered a heavy personal loss which appears to have imposed some limit upon the range of his efforts.

The King was out riding on his pony last Tuesday [January 14—an error of dating ; it should have been Wednesday, January 15]. Next day the first signs of his present illness were observed. Later, the strain imposed by the bronchial attack upon the heart and blood vessels occasioned his doctors' uneasiness. His Majesty was 63 when he suffered from septicaemia ; he is now 70. In the circumstances anxiety was and is inevitable. It must persist until the existing strain upon the heart has been relieved.

To the above statement must be subjoined another which appeared in the *British Medical Journal* after the fatal termination of the illness. This said :

Though it is understood that for some weeks His Majesty's health had not been altogether satisfactory, the King was able to go out, and

5

in fact rode on his pony for a short time on Wednesday, January 15. On Thursday, January 16, the King showed signs of a mild catarrh, which soon began to abate.

The " disquiet " expressed on Friday and Saturday arose from evidences of cardiac insufficiency. The margin of cardiac reserve had in recent days been narrowing. This illness therefore arose from within, and was in the nature of a culmination. It was thus not comparable to the invading streptococcal septicaemia localizing at the base of the right lung from which King George suffered seven years ago. That illness inevitably placed heavy burdens on the heart, and therefore may have had a causal relationship to this last illness.

It is a remarkable achievement for King George to have recovered from septicaemia and then to have reigned over his Empire for seven years through times which have been eventful and sometimes anxious. This last brief chapter of the King's life showed that the body carried through its work till its powers were ended and then came to rest after an illness short and peaceful in its close.

And to this should be appended the following tribute to Lord Dawson of Penn, King George's physician, paid by the *Lancet* :

It is fitting for members of the medical profession, who know from experience the keen anxiety attached to the care of a patient whose cardiac reserve is slight and whose duties are onerous, to voice the gratitude of the Empire to Lord Dawson of Penn, on whom for eight years a heavy burden has fallen. It must have been due in no small part to his constant unobtrusive watchfulness, as well as to his clinical wisdom, that these years were for King George years of joyous fulfilment.

Saturday, January 18, therefore, found the British people hushed and fearful, though hope had not gone. All thoughts were with the King and his family. It was a frosty morning, the earth snow-powdered, with glints of deceiving sunshine. Very early people from villages near the King's home made their way to the gates of Sandringham House to glean what information there might be. In London crowds gathered outside Buckingham Palace. Throughout the Empire people waited by their wireless sets, and the B.B.C. were admirably awake to the service of the public ; their headquarters became, when the newspaper presses were silent, the chief staple of news ; the fountain head of intelligence during that and the succeeding days of misgiving was

6

reached by tuning in to " National " ; it was the link between the world and that sick room at Sandringham. Three bulletins were issued. They were as follows :

JANUARY 18, 10.15 A.M. :
The anxiety expressed in the bulletin of last night persists.

3.30 P.M. :
His Majesty the King has had some hours of restful sleep. The cardiac weakness and the embarrassment of the circulation have slightly increased and give cause for anxiety.

10 P.M. :
There is no change to report since the last bulletin was issued.

The tension was increased by the knowledge that Sir Maurice Cassidy, the heart specialist, had temporarily joined the other doctors at Sandringham—Sir Frederic Willans, Sir Stanley Hewett, and Lord Dawson of Penn, and his signature appeared with theirs on the afternoon bulletin.

Sunday dawned in a dejection of spirit and weather in London, although in the neighbourhood of Sandringham the sun at least opposed in brightness the general anxiety. Many Norfolk residents waited by the gates of the King's house for further bulletins. Some walked or drove on towards the beautiful parish church of St. Mary Magdalene, just within the park, on the north side. Here the King was wont to worship when in residence at Sandringham ; that Sunday the Royal pew was empty. Those who gathered near the church noted sadly that none of the Royal Family attended the service. The service was conducted by the Rev. A. R. Fuller, rector of Sandringham, whose sermon was based on the text " Casting all your care upon Him." He spoke of the way in which those who cast their cares on God were helped in their prayers for the King and thus received support in their anxiety. The rector said he had been authorized to state that the King was slightly stronger than he had been yesterday. The sermon was followed by special prayers for the King, the Queen, and all the members of the Royal Family, and for the doctors and nurses in attendance on His Majesty. The hymns were " Father of all, to Thee with loving hearts we pray " and " Christ is our corner-stone." The announcement made by the

7

rector that the King was slightly stronger was received with relief, for the bulletin issued the night before had increased concern.

Only two bulletins were issued on that Sunday of January 19. They were as follows :

11 A.M. :

In spite of a restless night, His Majesty the King has maintained strength.

7.15 P.M. :

His Majesty the King has passed a quiet day. There is no change in His Majesty's condition.

Much interest was taken in the comings and goings between London and Sandringham. One of those who attracted special attention on arrival at King's Lynn on Sunday evening was the Archbishop of Canterbury, friend of the King for nearly half a century. He was met at the station by a Royal car and taken to Sandringham House. During the afternoon the Duke of Kent arrived, but the Prince of Wales and the Duke of York returned to London, arriving together at York House. The Prince of Wales went to No. 10, Downing Street at 4.30 and was with the Prime Minister for about three-quarters of an hour. Later, the Lord Chancellor called there, and remained with Mr. Baldwin about the same length of time. The Prince afterwards saw the Duke and Duchess of Gloucester at Buckingham Palace. He remained in London that night and returned to Sandringham on the Monday.

The Duke of York went on from London to Windsor, where the Duchess was recovering from her illness. He travelled from London by car, arriving at Royal Lodge, Windsor Great Park, soon after 4.30. There he was joined by Princess Helena Victoria, who had driven over in order to hear direct from the Duke the latest news of the King's condition. The Duke remained at Windsor that night, and returned to Sandringham next morning. Princess Elizabeth and Princess Margaret Rose, who left Sandringham on Saturday after the grave nature of the King's illness had become apparent, travelled to Windsor by car on the Sunday morning, and remained with their mother at Royal Lodge.

8

The Duke and Duchess of Gloucester were compelled to stay in London, where the Duke had recently been confined to his room at Buckingham Palace suffering from a sore throat.

Throughout Sunday large crowds gathered, as they had on Saturday, outside the main gates of Buckingham Palace. The constant coming and going of private motor-cars and taxi-cabs and the anxious demeanour of all sorts of people who arrived to learn the latest official news recalled the similar scenes when the King lay ill in the Palace in the winter of 1928.

It was not until just before noon that they saw published the further statement that in spite of a restless night the King had maintained strength. When this further announcement was posted there was an eager rush of people to read it, and the police had to move on those who had seen it so that others might get near. The crowd rapidly increased as the church services ended, and the Guardsmen on sentry-go outside the Palace often had difficulty in marching up and down. To relieve the traffic congestion police officers conveyed the substance of the announcement to motorists as soon as they pulled up.

In spite of the cold and foggy weather crowds of people waited about throughout the afternoon for further news. With its bare flag-pole and with the blinds drawn at most of the windows the Palace presented few signs of activity, but motor-cars arrived and left occasionally. When a copy of the evening bulletin from Sandringham was posted there was again a rush of people to read it, and much relief was expressed that there was no worsening of the King's condition. By this time the crowd was smaller, but the bulletin had been awaited for some time by scores of people who stood about in a drizzle of rain. Throughout the evening motorists continued to drive up to the Palace gates to learn the latest news.

Churches throughout the Empire offered prayers for the King's recovery on the Sunday as they had done on the Saturday. Speaking in Canterbury Cathedral on Saturday, the Archbishop of Canterbury had said :

It would be foolish to deny that there are grounds of anxiety, but there are also good grounds of hope in the King's proved powers of recovery, in the knowledge, experience, and skill of his doctors and nurses. I am sure that the love and loyalty which were so wonderfully manifested last year, in the King's Jubilee Year, will be expressed now by the prayers of all his people that the Holy Spirit, the Lord and Giver of Life, may bring to him full strength and recovery, may give trust and confidence to the Queen, and may give wisdom and skill to those who have care of him. Let us all pray that a life which means so much to this realm may be restored to full health and strength.

At the morning services at Westminster Abbey and other places of worship on Sunday a minute's silence was observed immediately after the sermon, while the congregation prayed for the King's restoration to health. Similar incidents marked the day in every country of the Empire and in the United States. Messages conveying their wishes for the King's recovery came from the heads of foreign countries, including the King of Italy, the French President and Herr Hitler. In Dublin anxious inquiries arrived at frequent intervals at the newspaper offices, and the great majority of wireless sets were tuned in to receive the B.B.C. bulletins. In the news bulletins of the Irish Free State broadcasting service the latest announcement regarding His Majesty's illness was the first item to be broadcast. Mr. Lansbury testified to the feelings of the Labour Party in a speech at Castleford, Yorkshire, in which he said : " our hearts go out to all who suffer, especially to the King, not because his sufferings will be any greater or any less than those of other people, but because he is the central figure in the country and the whole of the British Dominions."

Rain, with fitful interludes of sunshine, on Monday, January 20, marked a day that ended in national bereavement. The mingled emotions of hope and inquietude found expression in the following leading article, entitled *Vivat Rex*, which appeared in *The Times* that morning :

The clear, strong tones of the broadcast Christmas message were still ringing in our ears, and farther away and fainter, but not yet lost, were the cheering and the pealing bells and all the glad music of the Jubilee, when there fell over all the hush of the sick-room. The suddenness of it took the breath away. Scarcely was it known that the King had a cold when, with the candour that is the due of his subjects' love, his doctors spoke ominous words. The King had borne the fatigue of the Jubilee so robustly, and the news of his health since then had been so notably the no news which is good news, that his illness of seven years ago was almost forgotten. Now far and wide over the world

This now famous picture of King George at the microphone at Sandringham was taken by a staff photographer of *The Times*.

flashed the word " disquiet," to be followed by the graver word " anxiety." And from far and wide over the world flashed back the proofs of the deep concern which the news was causing.

There is no man alive to whom more hearts and minds in all the nations of the world wish health and strength than King George of England ; and to us, to his own peoples, he has grown so close that to each and all his illness is a poignant personal distress, from which flows, in all strength and simplicity of feeling, the keenest personal sympathy with his devoted wife, our Queen. Not to face the facts would be cowardly. Yet so vast is the volume of desire for the King's recovery ; from so many temples of religion, from so many of the great ones and of the governing assemblies of the nations, from the hearts of so many humble men, women, and children goes up the prayer that, not for his own sake but for his Empire's sake and the world's sake, the life of this good man may be spared, that to hope on is a work of wisdom as well as of duty to our King and our friend.

That sombre day will live in history as one that marked the final integration of broadcasting with our social life. Their intimate welding was the symbol of the intimate welding of all hearts in the widespread British domains. The morning service of the B.B.C. had its theme in an expression of spiritual comfort to " Mary, our Queen, the Royal Family, and the subjects of our King during these anxious days." The clergyman conducting said : " In our morning prayers during these anxious days we shall not keep rigidly to official programme announcements." After the hymn " Shepherd Divine, our watch relieve" had been sung, a prayer was said containing the petition : " Deal graciously we pray Thee, with all who are anxious at this time, especially Thy servant Mary our Queen, the Royal Family, and the subjects of our King in all parts of the world, who, by casting their care on Thee, may know the greatness of Thy strength and the consola-tion of Thy love." A prayer " for all who are in pain " followed, and the hymn " O Lord, how happy should we be If we could cast our care on Thee " was sung.

A few hours later a feeling which made a paradoxical alliance of insecurity and hope was raised by the first bulletin, issued at 10.45 a.m. It said :

The King has had a more restful night. There is no substantia change to record in His Majesty's condition.

II

But the succeeding hours were full of strain. In the afternoon the following official statement was issued from the Privy Council Office :

His Majesty the King, at a Council held at Sandringham this morning, appointed Counsellors of State.

Those so appointed are :

> HER MAJESTY THE QUEEN,
> H.R.H. THE PRINCE OF WALES,
> H.R.H. THE DUKE OF YORK,
> H.R.H. THE DUKE OF GLOUCESTER, and
> H.R.H. THE DUKE OF KENT.

There were present at the Council the Archbishop of Canterbury, the Lord Chancellor, the Lord President of the Council, Lord Dawson of Penn, Lord Wigram, and the Home Secretary.

Sir Maurice Hankey was in attendance as Clerk of the Council.

Members of the Privy Council had travelled from London to attend the meeting of the Council at Sandringham. Mr. MacDonald (Lord President of the Council), Lord Hailsham (Lord Chancellor), Sir John Simon (Home Secretary), and Sir Maurice Hankey (Clerk to the Privy Council) arrived at Wolferton station shortly after 11.30, and entered a Royal car, which conveyed them to Sandringham House. The Prince of Wales and the Duke of York returned from London by air to Bircham Newton, and thence drove to Sandringham.

The meeting of the Privy Council was held in the sitting-room adjoining the King's sick room, a connecting door being left open in order that His Majesty might follow the proceedings, which must be carried out in his presence. The Order in Council appointing the Queen and the four Royal Princes as Counsellors of State was handed to the King for signature by Lord Dawson of Penn, who is a Privy Councillor. His Majesty having approved, although his remaining strength was not sufficient to sign his name, Royal power was vested in the Counsellors of State. The Archbishop of Canterbury and Lord Wigram, who are members of the Privy Council, were present. In a later chapter this poignant scene is described in the words of the Archbishop of Canterbury and the Home Secretary in the course of the tributes they made in Parliament to the memory of King George.

12

Mr. MacDonald, Lord Hailsham, Sir John Simon, and Sir Maurice Hankey left Sandringham House about half-past two and drove to the aerodrome at Bircham Newton, where the three Ministers boarded an aeroplane to fly back to London. There was no room for Sir Maurice Hankey in the machine, so he went on to Wolferton and travelled back to London by train. The Duchess of Kent arrived at Sandringham in the afternoon, having travelled by train to Wolferton. There was brilliant sunshine during the afternoon, and the Queen, the Princess Royal, and other members of the Royal Family walked in the grounds for a short time after luncheon. Throughout the day people waited near the main gates of Sandringham House anxious for news of the King's condition.

By evening the life of London was stilled. Music and dancing in public places ceased ; the streets were quiet. Only near Buckingham Palace was there any activity, and there it was muffled and solemn. Until after midnight people waited for news, though there were hours when the rain poured. But it may be that to those who stayed at home the night will be most memorable. Those who waited upon the wireless felt they were living through moments isolated in history. Not an odd angle of the isle, not a corner of the vast Empire, but had, in the beautiful instruction of George Herbert, " tuned its instruments," though for sadder purposes. Indeed, all the world listened. The bulletin issued at 5.30 had left hope abandoned. It read :

The condition of His Majesty the King shows diminishing strength.

The King lay dying ; there was no more to be done, or feared, or wished, but only a vigil to be kept. At 9.30 was read the most touching bulletin ever penned. It had been issued at Sandringham House at 9.25 :

The King's life is moving peacefully towards its close.

FREDERIC WILLANS.
STANLEY HEWETT.
DAWSON OF PENN.

At once the B.B.C. programme was stopped. All rooms were mute, and speaking became a sort of sacrilege while the inevitable moment approached. The wireless formed an indissoluble tie between home and palace and listeners felt in the presence of a loved friend on the confines of the next world. All knew what sight could not report. At 10 o'clock the haunting phrase, " the King's life is moving peacefully towards its close," again came through the air, followed by the broadcast of a five-minutes' service of recollection—the brave words of the twenty-third Psalm and a prayer for the King, the Royal Family, and for the nation. In the reawakening of barbaric thoughts over so large a part of Europe, he who was passing stood for the good pilot who steers in the storm, symbol of our guard against the traps and entangle-ments of social change, the stability of achievements hard won and cherished, the proof and touchstone of our hopes for the world. Every quarter of an hour the simple accents of the pen-ultimate bulletin rang sadly as a dirge ; and as the announcer's voice ceased all could hear the fateful strokes of the metronome measuring the minutes of life. At last the final announcement :

Death came peacefully to the King at 11.55 p.m. to-night in the presence of Her Majesty the Queen, the Prince of Wales, the Duke of York, the Princess Royal, and the Duke and Duchess of Kent.

> **FREDERIC WILLANS.**
> **STANLEY HEWETT.**
> **DAWSON OF PENN.**

For us a new reign would begin on the morrow, and all that that involves of a new life ; seasons would return ; but not for that good man would return day.

LEADING ARTICLES FROM "THE TIMES"

KING GEORGE V

THE vast community of lands and peoples united under the British Crown is one in its loss and one in its grief to-day. It mourns the Sovereign who has reigned over it these twenty-five years. It mourns the man who bore with simple and serious devotion the responsibilities confided to him early in life by his brother's unexpected death, who never forgot and never cheapened one obligation of his rank and office, and, throughout a reign crowded as never before with great cares and great issues, was unswervingly true to the confidence that all his peoples so freely gave him. Uppermost, wherever in the normal rhythm of their life the mourners go about the streets to-day, will be the sense of shock and deprivation. Yet close upon it must press, in every mind, a certain thankfulness not to be denied its entry into the void of loss. With the accents of his last broadcast still echoing, there must come vividly to every one—and, we may surely hope, to Her Majesty not least—the memory of the Jubilee. It is credibly recorded, and it is wholly characteristic of the King's modesty, that the surge of grateful loyalty and personal affection which greeted him last year on May 6 and in the weeks that followed was, in its eager warmth and vigour, utterly unexpected by the King himself. Though he was not of those whose natures yield easily to the emotions, the experience left him hardly able to speak of it afterwards without showing how deeply he had been touched and how profoundly, humbly even, he had responded to the only reward that it was in his people's power to offer him. There is happiness, at least, in remembering that the life so sorely threatened in 1928 was spared not only for seven years of new and incomparable service to the community, but also for the exhilaration of those days of sunlit rejoicing, accomplishment, and recompense.

His subjects' sorrow is, as their joy was, their instinctive tribute of honour to a life that accepted and transmits the high Victorian concept of private and public duty. In many tongues they will

C

have one message of hope and comfort for the Queen and her children, springing from a fellowship of loss that, as her own heart has ever been quick to prove, excludes no family and no home. The Crown at all times is the single institution that liberates and harmonizes the diversities of our State. " Past our devisal," it is, in equal and inseparable shares, a bond of policy and a bond of affection. It applies an overriding dimension to the divisions of space and time, creed and colour, climate and tradition, transmuting the whole into civilized power. What touches the Throne touches the Empire in every part. Here is reason why the unhoped-for news, racing through the streets of metropolitan cities and eddying out over the great spaces, should hush, as it will to-day, all other topics, and point the truth of Lord Balfour's dictum that " the King is everybody's King." And yet it is not reason enough. The Crown, save in constitutional text-books, never has been and never can be an abstraction. The theory and the symbol presume human truth as well as constitutional fact. It is the human truth which has been heard from all lips during the last anxious days and is now told in the grief of all sorts and conditions in all latitudes.

History, which now prefers to construct its chapters in movements rather than in reigns, will nearly be able to blend the old practice with the new when it comes to the years of King George V. They have all the natural markings of a definite historical phase. His reign has been a bridge whose abutments lie on a hither and a farther bank at a distance far greater than twenty-five years will ordinarily measure. His subjects may look back over the deeps they have crossed with their King, and reflect upon all that contrasts the lively but apprehensive world of 1910 with the sobered and inquiring world of 1935. Men still short of middle age can say that they have witnessed the work of more than a generation. They have seen the dynastic diplomacy of the old century spend itself in blood on the battlefields of the new. They have watched the whole political balance of the planet moving. They have lived through the constitutional adolescence of the British Empire. They have seen the British electorate trebled and the political emancipation of women carried through. They can compare of their own knowledge the remote ardours of politics before the War with to-day's patient and hardly combative search for the outline of economic salvation. Within little more than two decades the internal combustion engine and the invention of wireless telegraphy have worked out before their eyes a revolution by land, sea, and air comparable to that which George Stephenson began.

Is there a parallel for this compression of history, this acceleration of time, in a reign that has already begun to rank by itself as the second " Georgian era " ? Let a question be put to anyone who has witnessed to this turbulent tide of events, or, indeed, whose memory goes back beyond them, which of our institutions has best proved its rooted stoutness and answers most readily to the expectation of a new age. The most ancient of them all is still the youngest in the vigour which it draws increasingly from the need and the affection of democracy. In its great emotional moments the nation turns more than ever to the monarchy as the focus and expression of its unity, to an institution not so much raised above it as set firmly and intelligibly in its midst. In time of danger, as in time of rejoicing, the feet of Londoners and the thoughts of millions besides have learnt to flock to Buckingham Palace, instinctively seeking the visible meeting-point of their resolution or their joy, each man relying the more upon himself and upon his neighbour for the knowledge that all his care and all his pride are the King's no less than his. The human bond between Crown and people has been wrought afresh with no conquest of statecraft, of pre-eminent personality, or of the outward brilliance that may captivate popular favour for a time. Much less precariously it holds because King George and Queen Mary never failed to be in themselves and in all that surrounded them an unstudied example of good citizenship at its highest and simplest, and because the word " home " meant for them exactly what it means for the most home-loving of their subjects. The last revealing years of his reign might serve for its epitome and for his epitaph. Even his subjects hardly knew the whole of their debt until it was told them seven years ago by his danger and their own distress, and by his joy and theirs in the year of jubilee.

High-flown formalities would be inept and inadequate to describe King George's peculiar service to his House and realm. As Sovereign he has founded no masterful legend such as flourishes more sturdily with every new document from Queen Victoria's long life. It was not his to exert King Edward's influence on the imagination of foreign peoples and on the course of international diplomacy. But he leaves his own legacy from the most critical times, within and without, that his country has known—a model of courage, industry, common sense, and scrupulous constitutional practice. In all his actions he applied the strictest and most modern theory of the Royal function, and with him a finally settled and unambiguous tradition of constitutional duty may be said to begin. At its opening his reign was beset by the embarrassments of a political crisis unprecedented for eighty years. He was the King who gave his assent—and there are few left in these days to question its propriety—to the creation of peers at need to pass the Parliament Bill. Three years later, under the wider shadow of looming war, his summons brought the party leaders into conference under his roof in search of a compromise that should banish the threat of civil conflict. They were difficult and wearing times —for no man more so than for a conscientious Sovereign—and they have passed leaving the Crown as much above the battle as it has ever been. The years after the War brought other political change. When for the first time the Labour Party furnished him with advisers, its accession to office had nowhere a more courteous and more confident welcome than from the King. If the loyalty and precision of his regard for the Constitution are outstanding marks of his reign, so also is the careful and accurate anticipation of public opinion which invariably characterized his initiative. It may be variously illustrated, whether in his choice of a Prime Minister from the Lower rather than from the Upper Chamber on the death of Mr. Bonar Law, or in the graceful award of Lord Oxford's peerage as his personal gift, or again, and most notably, when with perfect constitutional propriety he invited that concentration of political strength which became the National Government and gave the country the means to accomplish a decisive act of self-discipline and to restore its fortunes in the very moment of disaster.

In leadership of the community generally the King spared himself nothing. Ministers may lay down their responsibilities— the King never. There is no question of the tax which the unending cares of his office laid upon a constitution never robust, nor of the difficulty with which he was from time to time persuaded, even after his illness, to intermit any of his duties. In 1931 he was characteristically the first to make his own generous contribution to the alarming necessities of that time. His spontaneous example headed every appeal during the War for sacrifice in things great and small. And it was the same unresting sense of duty, the same loyal qualities which guided him impeccably in affairs of State, that first gave him his personal hold upon the affection of the solid mass of his subjects at home and oversea. The annals of the monarchy, of course, can show other titles to personal popularity. There was no mistaking the contrast of type between the late King and his father. His subjects" appreciation of King Edward owed much to their feeling that he was " one of them " in many of his likes and dislikes, a free and generous as well as a gifted spirit who took his full share in various forms of popular enjoyment. The instinct of the man-in-the-street rallied easily to him. King George's community with the national spirit was not less intimate, but it was in the other and more serious tradition. It was the bond of homely things and homely standards prized in common by the King and by innumerable households throughout the Empire. There was nothing cosmopolitan in his tastes. No Englishman had a firmer prejudice in favour of his own land and familiar surroundings or a heartier pleasure in them. Not that the King, as his subjects saw him, lacked other claims to the respect and affection of an inveterately sporting people. He certainly shared one taste with his faithful commons in his enjoyment of Rugby and Association football. His colours, it goes without saying, were immensely popular on the Turf. He was known as a devotee of the open air, as a keen yachtsman, and as one of the half-dozen best game-shots in his kingdom. But it is hardly in this direction that a biographer will seek the clues to character and the reasons why each and all, high and low, feel themselves poorer in this day of loss. He will turn, rather, to the earlier years.

King George was not placed in direct succession to the Throne until he was 27. His training till then had been in the Navy, and he was immersed in and proud of his profession. He absorbed the essential spirit of a Service career, and he has not been the first to prove it a true foundation for a career of service. The sea sense of duty, order, and thoroughness seemed to ring in the decisive, resonant tones of his speaking voice. When he went among his people they could not fail to recognize his key-qualities. His addresses were sincere and to the point. He knew, as well as any of his hearers, as thoroughly as his Ministers, the character of the times and the character of the tasks before us. His visits to industrial districts were not ceremonial, nor were his questions to managers, foremen, and others perfunctory. The study of these things began to interest him very early in life, and it was with his usual conscientious care that he acquired an unusual mastery of their scope and detail. He owed other things, too, to his Service experience. The Navy began for him nearly fifty years ago that series of voyages which has only been surpassed in his family by his son and successor. In the fullness of time the King came to the Throne an expert second to none in the knowledge of his Empire. For him, as it will be for the new King, his wide realm was not a map but a living thing in three dimensions, seen and studied ; and to his heir, as to him, every part of his Dominions will offer more than constitutional courtesies—a vivid, flesh-and-blood loyalty. A reign of great deeds, great sufferings, great perils, and great splendour is ended, and the name of King George V is added to the illustrious roll of those who have loved and lived for their country.

The Lying-in-State at St. Mary Magdalene Church, Sandringham.

THE QUEEN

IT is quite certain that, next to the sense of personal loss, the uppermost feeling in the minds of all peoples of the Empire is one of sympathy and admiration for Queen Mary. For forty-two years as Duchess of York and Cornwall, Princess of Wales and Queen, she has enjoyed the happiness of an ideal union and has set an example to her husband's subjects which (particularly in the disordered years following the War) has been of incalculable value to the national life. Looking back into the past, those who seek for a parallel may perhaps find it best in the case of King George III and Queen Charlotte. The example of their happy domestic life did more than anything else to establish the Monarchy in the hearts of the people and to enable it to withstand the revolutionary disturbances of the early nineteenth century. So it has been with King George and Queen Mary. While neighbouring monarchies have fallen, they have strengthened the English Monarchy and enhanced its prestige.

To the casual observer the tasks of a Queen Consort may seem merely formal and simple—though they are tasks which no one would lightly undertake. Driving in State processions, opening public buildings, and attending charitable functions—the outward and visible signs of Royalty—these have no doubt played their part in establishing the Queen in the affections of the public ; but her popularity is based on something far deeper—the knowledge that ceremonial and public appearances have not been the sum total of her service to the State, but that she has devoted her life to supporting her husband's work. In a memorable letter to the Duke of Wellington Prince Albert thus summed up his views as to the duties and position of a Prince Consort : " The husband should entirely sink his *own individual* existence in that of his wife —that he should aim at no power by himself or for himself— should shun all contention—assume no separate responsibility

23

before the public, but make his position entirely a part of hers."
The duties of a Queen Consort are no different. That the Queen
has exactly carried out that difficult advice, and filled her exalted
position to the admiration of every one, is familiar to us all,
and that the consciousness of it may sustain her will be the wish
of us all.

Unlike Queen Victoria, the Queen has not had to face widow-
hood after a comparatively short married life. King George and
Queen Mary were in fact married for exactly twice as long as
Queen Victoria and the Prince Consort, but the very length of the
companionship can only increase the sense of loss and feeling of
desolation. The certainty that these same feelings are shared by
millions of people throughout the world must do something, it
may be hoped, to console her, and many, as they mourn, will
remember those familiar comforting lines :

> The love of all Thy people comfort Thee
> Till God's love set thee at his side again.

CHAPTER II

AN EMPIRE IN MOURNING

O N the evening of January 21 the body of King George was taken from Sandringham House to the church of St. Mary Magdalene in the Park. The coffin, of Sandringham oak, from the same tree, grown on the King's estate, as that of the coffin of Queen Alexandra, was carried down from the death chamber by woodmen and gamekeepers of the estate, and at the door of the house was laid on the same hand bier that bore the coffin of Queen Alexandra ten years ago.

While these sad rites were in progress a King's Piper, Pipe Major Forsyth, played a lament under the window of King George's room. Twenty Grenadier Guardsmen who had arrived from London walked as escort beside the bier. As soon as everything was ready, the Queen, with members of her family, left Sandringham House and walked behind the coffin to the church in a shower of rain and sleet. The Duke of Kent and the Earl of Harewood walked with the Queen, and the Princess Royal and the Duchess of Kent followed.

The coffin was carried into the church by Guardsmen and set down in the chancel, and in the presence of the Royal mourners a brief service was conducted by the rector.

There, where King George had so often worshipped, his body now lay until, on January 23, it should be removed for the journey to London and the lying-in-state in Westminster Hall.

The same day King Edward left Sandringham to attend the meeting of the Privy Council in London. With the Duke of York he drove to Bircham Newton and continued the journey thence by air. Thus His Majesty, the first British Monarch to fly, early created a precedent.

Another change which was observed that morning was that the clocks at Sandringham now showed the right time. Hitherto they had been always kept half an hour fast since King Edward VII decreed that his should be done—as an incentive to punctuality, it is said, when his shooting parties met.

During the morning the Archbishop of Canterbury and Sir Stanley Hewett left Sandringham, returning to London by train. The Queen and those of her family who remained at Sandringham with her spent this first day of bereavement in a vigilantly guarded privacy. Across the iron gates which afford a view of the path leading from Sandringham House to the Church of St. Mary Magdalene a long canvas screen was spread.

Meanwhile it had been arranged that an opportunity should be given to King George's tenants and neighbours to take a last leave of him where he lay in the church of St. Mary Magdalene, and so on January 22 for six hours or more an irregular stream of visitors from near and far passed slowly through the narrow chancel so close to the Royal Standard which draped the coffin that they could have touched the bright gold leopards. A cross of white chrysanthemums and orchids from the Queen rested on the coffin at the head. Beside it was a simple wreath of red carnations and white chrysanthemums from King Edward and other members of the Queen's family. At each corner of the bier stood with bowed head one of the staff of the Sandringham estate.

There was a fine dignity in the quiet demeanour of the visitors, most of them country folk who live in the neighbourhood, but with a sprinkling who came out in motor-omnibuses from King's Lynn and other towns, or who parked their own cars outside the gates. They did not speak to one another above a whisper—most did not speak at all—as they moved along the nave and through the chancel. One long earnest look at the coffin as they passed by, and without pausing further they came out by the door at the east end. Many of the women wore black, and some of the men and children had a mourning band on the sleeve.

During the afternoon the Queen, with the Princess Royal, the Duke of Kent, and the Earl of Harewood, walked from Sandringham House to the church, which for some time was closed to the public.

King Edward arrived at Sandringham from London on the evening of that day. He travelled by train to Wolferton, where a Royal car waited to convey him to Sandringham House. With the King were the Duke and Duchess of York and the Duke and Duchess of Gloucester. On alighting from the train they immediately entered the car and drove to Sandringham. The darkness prevented the people lined up on the roadside from recognizing the occupants of the cars, but respectfully they stood in silence, the men with bared heads.

Soon after his arrival King Edward, accompanied by the Duke of Gloucester, visited the church.

The note of mourning swelled beyond Sandringham and England to embrace the Empire and the world. The news of King George's death reached Ottawa shortly after 7 p.m. on January 20, and was relayed by the radio stations and published in special editions of the newspapers. It spread swiftly to the remotest corners of the Dominion and evoked a spontaneous outburst of nation-wide sorrow and regret. The normal telephone staff in Ottawa and other places had to be increased by half to answer extra calls. Soon after the arrival of the news the great bell in the Peace Tower of Parliament Buildings began to toll, and the Canadian people everywhere, in every sphere of life, abandoned virtually all activities. Meetings of public bodies were adjourned, music and dancing in hotels stopped, taverns and restaurants closed their doors, and all signs of gaiety were banished. In the afternoon, when the ominous bulletin arrived, Mr. Mackenzie King, the Prime Minister, left the Cabinet meeting for Rideau Hall to confer with Lord Tweedsmuir.

As in London so in Ottawa, social activity ceased like a machine run down. The sorrow of the Canadian people found expression in a multitude of ways. " Unwonted quiet," said the Ottawa correspondent of *The Times*, " prevails everywhere, because the majority of people appear to be affected by a sense of deep personal loss."

To Australians not since the War had the consciousness of their share in the Empire been brought home with greater force than by the death of King George. The course of his illness was followed with extreme anxiety, but in their remote unawareness of the real facts Australians allowed their hopes to run high. The announcement of his death came as a stunning blow.

In all the capitals and provincial cities the newspapers issued editions within a few minutes of the receipt of the tidings, while the remotest townships, stations, and farms were informed through the radio. Flags were half-masted, public offices closed, and sports cancelled. One train leaving Melbourne for a country race meeting was recalled when it reached an outer suburb, and the meeting was abandoned. Theatres and cinemas everywhere closed.

Mindful of his recent visit to London, Mr. Lyons, the Prime Minister, said :

It is hard to realize that the man who was able to review with so alert a mind the vastness of his Empire is no more, that the hand which acknowledged the heart-felt cheers of multitudes is stilled, and that the face which so readily lit up into a smile of appreciation will never smile again. We learned during those wonderful days the reason for the universal respect and affection in which he was held by his people. We saw a King and a man, in both capacities, displaying qualities of the highest degree. He typified all that is best in the British character, and now he is dead at a time when the echoes of the Jubilee-year cheering have scarcely ceased. He goes to his last rest after a reign in which he led his people with wisdom, dignity, and devotion through perilous days. Australians, with the rest of the Empire, mourn the passing of a beloved monarch.

In New Zealand the solemn tolling of the big Bourdon bell of the Memorial Carillon named Reo Wairua, or the " spirit voice," informed Wellington of King George's death. The news was received just before the luncheon hour, and Government offices and business premises, where possible, were closed for the rest of the day. In a statement on behalf of the Government and people, Mr. Savage, the Prime Minister, expressed " deep emotion and distress " at the death of a " great man and a great leader." He added :

The Dominion joins in mourning the loss of a beloved Monarch. No man in modern times has so endeared himself to so many millions. During the War years and the years of depression he showed the deepest sympathy with his subjects in all their sufferings and distress. Indeed, throughout his reign he shared the cares and hopes of the humblest of his people. The Jubilee celebrations showed how deeply he was honoured as a leader and loved and respected as a man. He had revealed himself through numerous crises and through a long and illustrious reign as a man of great wisdom and character, and always as a simple, direct, and lovable personality. The deepest and most heartfelt sympathy of the people of the Dominion goes out to Her Majesty the Queen and the other members of the Royal Family.

The public throughout the Union of South Africa spontaneously observed January 21 as a day of mourning, while a Government *Gazette Extraordinary* was published announcing King George's death and proclaiming the day following as one of national mourning. All shops, offices, and places of entertainment were shut. Services were held in the churches, which remained open all day for those who wished to pray privately. A day of solemn prayer was observed in the Moslem community. To the Governor-General's office from all over the country—from the four Provincial Administrators to tiny backveld municipalities— came countless tributes to the dead monarch. In an eloquent address General Smuts said :

The passing of the King is an irreparable loss not only to our Commonwealth but to the whole world. His influence was one of the most beneficent forces for international good will. He was a beloved personality, and his broad and human sympathies endeared him to people all over the world. Americans especially vied with his own loyal subjects in attachment to him. To the League of Nations and all the human causes it stands for he was a firm friend. A great cementing and healing influence has passed away, and nothing can fill the gap his going has made.

The news of the King's death reached Delhi at 6.30 in the morning (local time), and through channels usual in India was known throughout the city within an hour, although special editions of newspapers did not appear until later. Men told the news to crowds coming out into the grey, rain-flecked morning from mosques and temples, where worshippers, after their ordinary prayers, had interceded for the King's recovery. Delhi, the capital of the Moghul Empire and of the Sultans, has been the scene of the deaths of many rulers attended by civil turmoil, but the death of George the Well-Beloved, whose Jubilee people were so recently joyfully celebrating, brought a feeling of universal deep sadness at the sudden passing of a great King whose solicitude for India was a household word.

The words *hamara badshah marghye* (" Our King is dead ") spread rapidly. Shops were closed ; Union Jacks that had been put away since the Jubilee were hoisted at half-mast on the houses and on the Fort from whose ramparts, after the Coronation Durbar, the King had appeared to his Indian people ; bells tolled at St. James's Church, where later was held a special service which was broadcast throughout India.

Many scenes were observed typical of the grief of ordinary Indians. A group of Gurkhas, ex-soldiers, walking to work, noticed a newspaper poster, stopped, saluted, and passed on discussing in low tones the death of the Monarch who is familiar almost as a personal friend to the Indian martial classes. Punjabi Moslems recalled how they had seen the King touring the Front in France. Hindu merchants remembered the Prince of Wales in Delhi, and said India would have another good King-Emperor. Newspaper biographies of King George were pondered over by groups of countrymen who stood round literate Indians as they explained them. Many public bodies met and passed resolutions of profound sorrow.

The Viceroy sent the following telegram to the Secretary of State for India :

The Government of India have heard with profound sorrow of the demise of His Majesty the King-Emperor. India mourns the death of a Sovereign whose Silver Jubilee was so recently celebrated with marks of deepest loyalty and affection and who has always been looked up to as a true and trusted friend of all classes and conditions of his people within his Indian Empire. On behalf of the Princes and People of India we request you to convey to His Majesty the King-Emperor and to Her Majesty Queen Mary this expression of our heartfelt sorrow, and to offer to His Majesty our respectful homage on his accession to the Throne of the British Empire.

With Lady Willingdon he attended a special service at the Church of the Redemption at New Delhi. In the cities markets, shops, offices, mills and places of education were closed. The Nizam of Hyderabad's Jubilee celebrations were postponed indefinitely. The Aga Khan declared that nowhere in the world would the death of King George be mourned more deeply than in India. And as in the great Dominions so in the remotest Colonies the voice of sorrow was upraised.

The news was received with the deepest emotion by the representatives of the many nations which are members of the League of Nations and was reflected in the moving ceremony which took place in the Council chamber. The regular business of the League was postponed for a day, and the Council meeting transformed into a brief memorial service in which each member of the Council in turn gave expression to the sympathy of his country in the loss that had befallen the Royal Family and the British people and its participation in their sorrow.

Mr. Bruce (Australia) presided over the gathering, which in outward form, and in all but the atmosphere of mourning, was that of a normal Council meeting. He expressed the sympathy of the Council for the Royal Family and the nation, and spoke with emotion of the personal qualities of the King, who had spent his life in the service of his people in a most difficult phase of the world's history, and had never wearied in his efforts for the cause of world peace and better understanding between the nations. The members of the Council, the Secretariat, the Press, and the public then rose and a moment's silence was observed.

M. Léger (representing France in the absence of M. Laval, who had already left for Paris) referred to the mourning of a great people which, under the high moral authority of its revered sovereign, had always been actively associated with the defence and organization of peace.

After further tributes had been paid by the delegates of Italy, Russia, Spain, Poland, Rumania, Denmark, Turkey, Argentina, Chile, and Ecuador, Mr. Bruce, as representative of one of the other nations of the British Commonwealth in the League, associated Australia with the tributes rendered to his late Majesty and the sympathy for Great Britain expressed by the nations assembled at the Council table. Mr. Eden, replying, said :

As the representative of H.M. Government in the United Kingdom, I wish to express to my fellow-members of the Council our deep appreciation of their expressions of sympathy on the occasion of the death of our beloved Sovereign George V. The Council will forgive the emotion with which I speak. To every one of his many millions of subjects throughout the world the death of His Majesty has brought a sense of heavy loss, to those whose proud duty it has been to serve him a deep and intimate sorrow.

31

We live in a time of storm and stress. We tread warily on shifting sands. But to us in my country there has been one sure rock—the personality of our King. Through all these troublous years he has stood, the symbol of all that we respect, the epitome of those qualities to which we as Englishmen aspire. Now he has left us. We mourn him deeply and sincerely. For we feel that we have lost in him not merely the ruler but the father of his people. He is dead, but he will live on in the hearts of his loyal and faithful subjects.

From you, this great council of the nations, my country has to-day received warm and generous sympathy. We mourn and you have mourned with us. For the words that you have spoken, for the sympathy that you have expressed, I tender to you, on behalf of the British people, our sincere and heartfelt thanks.

From the heads of States numerous messages of condolence were dispatched. President Roosevelt declared in a telegram to King Edward that King George occupied a " high and unique place " in the respect and affections of the people of the United States. In Germany many flags flew at half-mast, and Herr Hitler assured King Edward of his deep grief. M. Piétri, the French Minister of Marine, issued the following Order of the Day to be read to all ranks at sea and on land :

King George is dead. A great influence has vanished. The death-knell has echoed to the very limits of the world, and all the nations grouped around the British flag are plunged into mourning. We Frenchmen should never forget what the memory of this Prince means to us. He was our faithful friend and the puissant champion of a cause on which hung both the life and the destiny of France. You, sailors, be even more tender of his memory, for he was the supreme chief of those squadrons which, with ours and those of our Allies, assured the mastery of the seas and prepared the triumph of our arms. The Navies of our two countries unite to-day in grief as they have done in battle.

A great number of French people were filled with a feeling of almost intimate sorrow and loss. To them King George represented not only a great ideal of public service and personal dignity ; he stood also for the Great Britain of the War which stood loyally by her obligations to France and whose soldiers fought side by side with the soldiers of this country on French soil. He represented the consolidation and perfection

On the road from Sandringham to Wolferton Station.

of the Anglo-French *entente* which was happily founded by King Edward but met and withstood its supreme test in the reign of his son.

In the official world the death of King George was the occasion for the marks of respect due to the head of a friendly nation, with the added sincerity born of personal sympathy and the sense of close international ties. The appearance of Paris was that which it wears when a great leader of France has passed away. On every public building, by order of the Minister of the Interior, the Tricolor flew at half-mast ; in many cases the Union Jack flew with it, and each wore a draping of crêpe. The Senate and the Chamber both suspended their sessions for an hour in sign of mourning, after their presidents had paid tribute to the late King, to which Ministers replied.

In Brussels, Copenhagen, Vienna, Rome, indeed in the capitals of Europe and the world, the outward signs of mourning were repeated. The Italian wireless stations suspended their programmes for an hour and a commemorative address was given by the Marchese Imperiali, Italian Ambassador in London in 1914, and for many years. In Tokyo black-bordered editions of the newspapers, carried by runners with bells, announced King George's death an hour after it occurred. The English Royal House is the only one with which the Japanese Royal House has a tradition of personal friendship, and memories of the late King's kindness when the Emperor was visiting England and the present King's visit to Japan made the sympathy expressed on all sides more than a formal courtesy. On receiving the news the Emperor sent his Chamberlain with condolences to the British Ambassador and telegraphed to the King. Before proceeding to business both Houses of the Diet passed resolutions of condolence in silence, the members standing

And so, through the days following King George's death, by deed and word men of many races and creeds, men who spoke for nations and communities, men who spoke for families and for themselves, offered their tributes of sorrow and admiration, of affection and grief, until it became apparent that :

> "The shadow of His loss drew like eclipse,
> Darkening the World."

Meanwhile the march of events went on. King Edward, as has been stated, attended a meeting of the Privy Council held on

D

January 21 to proclaim his accession to the Throne. His declaration was published with other proceedings of the body in a Supplement to the *London Gazette Extraordinary*. In this he referred to " the irreparable loss which the British Commonwealth of Nations had sustained " by the death of his father, and continued :

" When my father stood here twenty-six years ago he declared that one of the objects of his life would be to uphold constitutional government. In this I am determined to follow in my father's footsteps and to work as he did throughout his life for the happiness and welfare of all classes of my subjects.

" I place my reliance upon the loyalty and affection of my peoples throughout the Empire, and upon the wisdom of their Parliaments, to support me in this heavy task, and I pray that God will guide me to perform it."

The Supplement also contained the proclamation of the new King, and recorded the taking by him of the oath relating to the security of the Church of Scotland.

The ceremonies of accession were carried a stage further next day. With the resounding pageantry belonging to the historic event King Edward VIII was proclaimed successively at St. James's Palace, Charing Cross, Temple Bar, and the Royal Exchange. The Officers of Arms proceeding through the streets in Royal carriages were escorted by Royal Horse Guards, the route was lined by troops, and though the proclamation, in accordance with custom, was made early in the day, great crowds gathered to follow the ancient and stately usage.

To command a view of the scarlet-draped balcony from which the King was first proclaimed, members of the general public had to reach St. James's Palace not long after the usual breakfast hour. But the morning was fine, exhilarating rather than cold, and the sun, not strong enough to disperse the mists clinging to the trees in the park, freshly gilded the diamond clock just visible over the battlements and set the angular old brick palace in a soft romantic haze. Since Friary Court and the road through Marlborough Gate had been cleared for ceremonial movements, late comers—and at a quarter to 9 one was already a late comer—found themselves in the larger part of the pavement crowd which was trying hard to look round the corner of a brick wall. Early comers standing opposite the recessed court had to withstand a good deal of pressure from a crowd which soon extended into and along the Mall.

But for the greater part of the period of waiting there was little to see either inside or outside the palace court. Shouted orders told that troops were taking up position in the Mall, but it was not until half an hour before the ceremony was to begin that four Royal trumpeters, gorgeous in the grey of the morning, rode into the quadrangle and were followed in quick succession by companies of Guards. One company fixed bayonets and deployed along the crowded pavement ; another mounted a guard of honour under the balcony with a band drawn up at right angles ; and the escort of Royal Horse Guards filled Marlborough Gate with colour.

But for those looking directly into the court the scene had not much colour. The Guards, wearing their greatcoats, contributed only a glint of steel and a line of pipeclay until their draped Colours were slowly paraded. Spectators wearing dark clothes appeared behind the battlements and in the windows of the palace, a few found places beneath the windows, and when officials of the College of Arms arrived all their splendour was concealed in motor-cars.

The ceremony began with no warning save that given by the clock. Two minutes before 10 a.m. the great square window on which all eyes were fixed became a mass of varied, quaint, and gorgeous colour, and the Officers of Arms came slowly on to the balcony which is associated with the first appearance of Queen Victoria to her people on the occasion of her proclamation. Two mace-bearers and the Royal trumpeters stood to the right and left of the Kings of Arms, Heralds, Pursuivants, and Serjeants at Arms. At the first stroke of the hour the golden-sleeved trumpeters lifted their instruments. A double fanfare rang out. The troops presented arms. There was complete silence when the trumpets ceased.

Then the first gun awoke echoes in St. James's Park, and, speaking through the noise of gunfire, Sir Gerald W. Wollaston, Garter Principal King of Arms, read the proclamation :

Whereas [he said] it hath pleased Almighty God to call to His Mercy our late Sovereign Lord King George the Fifth, of Blessed and Glorious Memory, by whose Decease the Imperial Crown of Great

35

Britain, Ireland, and all other His late Majesty's Dominions is solely and rightfully come to the High and Mighty Prince Edward Albert Christian George Andrew Patrick David; We therefore, the Lords Spiritual and Temporal of this Realm, being here assisted with these of His late Majesty's Privy Council, with Numbers of other Principal Gentlemen of Quality, with the Lord Mayor, Aldermen, and Citizens of London, do now hereby with one Voice and Consent of Tongue and Heart, publish and proclaim, That the High and Mighty Prince Edward Albert Christian George Andrew Patrick David, is now, by the Death of our late Sovereign of happy Memory, become our only lawful and rightful Liege Lord Edward the Eighth, by the Grace of God, of Great Britain, Ireland and the British Dominions beyond the Seas King, Defender of the Faith, Emperor of India : To whom we do acknowledge all Faith and constant Obedience, with all hearty and humble Affection ; beseeching God, by whom Kings and Queens do reign, to bless the Royal Prince Edward the Eighth with long and happy Years to reign over us.

The proclamation made, Sir Gerald Wollaston, standing to attention, cried " God Save the King." The Earl Marshal, the Duke of Norfolk, repeated the cry, and, with the guns still firing, the trumpeters sounded another fanfare and the Guards' band played the National Anthem. Voices from the crowd joined in singing the last verse of the anthem. So the historic ceremony ended, and soon the Royal carriages with their cavalry escort were swinging into the Mall on their way to Charing Cross, where the proclamation was again made, to be repeated at Temple Bar and the Royal Exchange in the presence of vast crowds of people.

At Temple Bar the burgesses of the City of London, through their Lord Mayor, exercised their ancient right of barring the passage of the King and his officers across the boundary where the City of London begins and the Royal City of Westminster ends. A silken cord stretched across the road was the symbolic barrier. There were fanfares, challenge and counter-challenge. The arresting cry of the City Marshal—" Who comes there ? " —as he advanced to the barrier to meet Bluemantle Pursuivant, rang out clearly to the crowds at the Law Courts and beyond. In the quietness, broken only by the restless movements of the horses, the Pursuivant demanded entrance to proclaim the King—a demand granted to him, but for the moment denied to his escort.

He was conducted to the Lord Mayor, who, with the Aldermen and Sheriffs in their scarlet gowns, was stationed outside the entrance to the Temple, and there he presented the Order in Council requiring the Proclamation of the King. But, even now, the barrier was not removed. There was a reminder by the Lord Mayor that, knowing the contents of " this paper," he had attended to perform his duty " in accordance with the ancient usages and customs " of the City ; and the reading aloud of the Order in Council. Only then did the Lord Mayor direct that the King's Officers of Arms should be admitted, and the red cord drawn aside.

Great gatherings also heard the proclamation read in cities and towns throughout the country. There were 30,000 at the ceremony in Cathays Park, Cardiff, 20,000 in the Town Hall Square, Sheffield, and there were big attendances also at Manchester, Brighton, Newport, Plymouth, and Reading. Snow fell thickly during the ceremony at Blackburn. The proclamation was also read at naval and military stations, and in H.M. ships throughout the world. On the days following the proclamation was read in Edinburgh, Glasgow, Belfast, Windsor and elsewhere, and in the Dominions and Colonies.

Peers and members of the House of Commons assembled at Westminster on January 21 and 22 to take the oath of allegiance to the new Sovereign. Though informal, the proceedings were marked by reserved dignity. In the House of Lords the most notable feature of the scene was the Throne at the end of the Chamber, on which are usually two chairs on high for the King and Queen and one chair lower for the Prince of Wales. Now only one chair was there, for the Prince had become King and has no Consort.

On January 23 Parliament in noble language paid homage to King George. The Prime Minister, in an oration worthy of the occasion, spoke of the increased spiritual power of the Crown and testified to the triumphant way in which King George met the challenge of swiftly changing times—a " great and humble man " whose sense of duty to his people amounted to genius.

In the House of Commons members who had taken the oath were early in their places and filled the Chamber from end to end. The public were not admitted, except into the Ladies' Gallery, before prayers, and their first sight of the House disclosed Canon Carnegie, who had conducted prayers, retiring slowly towards the door between the silent and crowded benches. Proceedings opened informally with the reading by the Speaker of a few more messages of sympathy received from foreign Parliaments, and his announcement of the procedure to be followed in Westminster Hall, whither the body of King George had been brought to lie in state. Meanwhile the Prime Minister rose from his place and made his way to the Bar. From that place, holding out a sheet of parchment, he cried in a loud, clear voice : " A message from His Majesty the King, signed with His Majesty's own hand." Then, at the Speaker's invitation, he began the Parliamentary history of the new reign by bearing the message to the Table, where it was received by the Clerk and handed to the Speaker, who rose and read it. The message was brief and telling. It associated the House of Commons with the new King's grief, recalled in a single sentence his father's life of service to his people, and declared that this example would be followed.

A murmur of approbation passed over the audience, and the Speaker called upon the Prime Minister. Mr. Baldwin, in accordance with ancient and felicitous usage, then moved an Address, which was treated as one for purposes of comment, but as divided into two for the purpose of being put to the vote ; it was, in fact, threefold in substance. The first part recorded " affectionate and grateful remembrance " of King George ; the second part expressed serene confidence that King Edward would " promote the happiness of all his people " ; and these two parts were welded into one Address. But a third part tendered the " condolence, reverence, and affection " of the Commons to Queen Mary, and a special delegation from all parties was appointed to convey it to her.

Speaking on this text, Mr. Baldwin rose to great heights of moving but restrained eloquence. He recalled that Simon de Montfort summoned the first Parliament to Westminster Hall some six and three-quarter centuries ago on January 20, the very date of King George's death. Thus was a link forged between the man who sowed the seed of democracy and who, even in his defeat, converted his conqueror, that first and greatest of the Edwards ; and the King, just dead, who had done so much to bring to terms democracy and monarchy. This concordat had made the temporal power of the Crown less, but its spiritual power greater. Mr. Baldwin also found another link with the past in Westminster Abbey, where the first Edward lay buried and where, he added significantly, the eighth Edward would be crowned.

The last three Sovereigns, each in his or her own way, had fortified their influence by some special force of character. King George's gift was a sense of duty which amounted almost to genius. It had enabled him to meet the challenge of difficult and swiftly changing times and to triumph so that all the world to-day acknowledged that it had lost an exemplar. Thank God this great and humble man knew before his death what his people thought of him. Thank God he fell asleep in the plenitude of his powers, peacefully, before pain had dimmed the acuteness of his mind or sapped the energy of his body. There was no memory of him except at his fine best.

Mr. Baldwin had only a reverent sentence for the sorrow of the Queen, for he felt that her memories were too sacred for more than the simplest and sincerest condolence. But for the new King he had the heartening reminder that he possessed experience and gifts different perhaps, but perhaps also richer, than any of his predecessors, those architects of the new kingship. Edward VIII would find the Constitution now entrusted to his keeping adaptable as ever to desirable change. There could therefore be unbounded confidence that he would establish the Throne more surely than ever on its only sure basis—the hearts of the people.

Mr. Attlee, who followed with the Opposition tribute, reached no lesser height of feeling and of sincerity. He reminded the House that he and all members spoke for the people, and testified that every humblest household felt that they had lost a friend in the late " great and well-loved King." In an age of transition, King George had been a rallying point for progress combined with stability. As the supreme exponent of constitutional kingship, he had accepted the Parliament Act, the rise of the Labour Party, and the independence of the Dominions. His presence and balance had kept far from this land the curse of mass hysteria leading to the deification of party dictators. Thus he had strengthened his Throne when the thrones of others were crashing. Hardly less happily notable was the fact that in an age of broadcasting he was an ideal broadcaster, who knew how to speak to his people, because he shared their every trial as they now shared the grief of his family. As for the new King, he had already given proof of the same great qualities ; and the prayer of all was that his reign might be long, prosperous, and peaceful.

Brief but deep applause marked the general appreciation of this speech, and it was renewed for Sir Archibald Sinclair's admirably concise tribute to a King who had been to his people as a father to his family.

The Speaker put the questions to the House. Each was greeted with the short sharp " Aye " of unanimity, and declared carried *nemine contradicente.*

On the motion of the Prime Minister, seven members were appointed to convey the Address of condolence to Queen Mary.

The House of Lords presented a memorable scene. Every seat, except a few behind the front Opposition bench, was occupied. The sombre uniformity of mourning dress worn by the temporal Peers and by the rows of Peeresses in the galleries was relieved by the gold embroidery on the Lord Chancellor's state robe and the Bishops' white lawn. On the steps round the now solitary Throne were seated Privy Councillors and sons of Peers. The King's message was read by the Lord Chancellor.

Lord Halifax moved the Addresses. He reviewed in brief outline the reign of one who was Sovereign and truly father to all owing him allegiance. It was doubtful whether any other King these islands had known had had his lot cast in times of such continuing difficulty at home and abroad. Ever faithful to the spirit of the Constitution, King George pointed the path of moderation when fires of party blazed dangerously. In war he inspired the will to endurance, and his encouragement inspired confidence in darkest days of industrial depression. There was no home under the British flag that did not feel his death as a personal loss. The first gentleman in the land, he taught that only he who served could rightly claim that title.

Turning from the reign which has ended to the one that has begun, Lord Halifax spoke of King Edward's wide sympathies, which had been deepened by direct contacts of inestimable worth. Most earnestly all would pray that his reign would be long and abundantly blessed. The speech ended with a moving passage in which respectful sympathy was tendered to Queen Mary.

Lord Snell, the Leader of the Opposition, followed with a sincere tribute to the late King's courageous devotion to duty. He had given an inspiring example of dignity, simplicity, and fidelity to exacting responsibilities. The Labour Party honoured King George as a Head of the State who was an impartial friend to all and the chief servant of his people. In return they gave him full, spontaneous, and never-varying loyalty. The new King, whose careful preparation for his great task had been watched with keen interest, was assured of the understanding sympathy and trust of his people.

Lord Mottistone, speaking for the Liberal Peers in place of Lord Crewe, who was absent through illness, recalled the help and inspiration which the Army derived from King George's visits to the Western Front during the War and the kindly solicitude of the Queen in the hospitals.

The last tribute was paid by the Archbishop of Canterbury, who closed on a touching note. He described the King's devotion to duty when at noon on the last day of his life he sat, propped up in his chair at Sandringham, frail and weak, and received his last Privy Council with a kindly and kingly smile. He also spoke of the Queen's wonderful fortitude and calmness in bereavement, and expressed the hope that she would long be spared to her people.

The text of the speeches is reproduced elsewhere in this volume.

LEADING ARTICLES FROM "THE TIMES"

AN ENGLISHMAN'S RELIGION

"OUR most religious and gracious King" is a phrase in the prayer for the High Court of Parliament which has been used since 1662. If loyalty rather than veracity applied the first of those adjectives to the King then reigning, veracity no less than loyalty finds in it a true description of the Monarch we mourn to-day. There can be no hyperbole in terming "most religious" one whose religion was the very basis of his character and conduct. King George, indeed, showed at its best what may be described as a typically English attitude towards the Christian faith. It is a religion much inclined to reticence and reserve, due in part to a deep sense of awe in the presence of holy things, and in part to a dread of pose and sentimentalism. It is little versed in, and probably undervalues, the contribution which theology can make to spiritual life. Though it welcomes dignity in public worship at all times, and ceremonial stateliness on high occasions, it has a strong and almost instinctive aversion from elaborated fussiness of ritual. If it seems rather impervious to fresh knowledge, it is also admirably tenacious of ancient habits, and no change of fashion will detach it from its Sunday churchgoing, its private prayers, its Bible-reading. Religion of this type often finds noble expression in a life of duty-doing. Anyone who faces duty in the light of such a creed will find in it, not a mere impersonal code which he must obey, but a God-given opportunity which he can use.

In his religion, as in much else, our late King was a typical Englishman, and his working creed was not dissimilar to that here outlined. Each of the innumerable tributes to his memory at this time will rightly insist upon his complete devotion to duty. Yet they must draw a false portrait if they ascribe this characteristic chiefly to the tradition he inherited, or to his early training in the Navy, or, indeed, to any other source than his firmly held religious

45

faith. The utter self-forgetfulness with which he set himself daily to accomplish the daily task, the unwearied search for opportunities of showing kindness, were the direct consequences of his religion. He could not think of the two parts of life except in this direct relationship. It was his first duty, he held, to be religious, and the first product of any religion that was worth while must be consistent duty-doing. Then, and not otherwise, he could rely on Divine aid in his tremendous task. All who, less than a month ago, heard King George's Christmas message, will recall that " God help him " as he spoke of himself, and its impressive sincerity. Who can but feel to-day that the prayer has been answered ? The help which strengthened him throughout his reign, which kept his courage unbroken through its darkest days, which prolonged his life so that he might have in full measure the reward of his people's love, did not fail him at the end. It spared him, what alone he dreaded, another long illness or the disabilities of old age. A happy Christmas with his family in the setting he loved best, a swift passage through the shadow, and so home. God helped him, and that right early.

KING EDWARD VIII

YESTERDAY King Edward VIII received the allegiance of his Privy Council at St. James's Palace, made the declaration and took the oath which complete the act of accession, and to-day will be proclaimed with traditional ceremony by the Heralds. A new reign opens, as age-long precedent requires, upon a page of stately illumination that records the long descent of an ancient trust, and sheds for a moment the jewelled light of the Middle Ages upon the inheritance of the King's Dominions. The King is dead. Long live the King. Yet to most minds the constitutional truth preserved in the ancient and honoured formula has not been the first among the reflections which it brought. What it brought home to them rather was the burden of duty which their service lays upon a King, the all-absorbing claims which must dominate the first hours of kingship and end only with life itself. It would have been dullness of soul indeed to have failed to couple, in their moving significance, the last act of State in the reign now ended with the instant public call to the new King in the hour when, if ever, human nature may crave a consoling respite for its thought and its memories.

King Edward VIII comes to the Throne as no stranger to his peoples. Few, very few, of his subjects can rival the knowledge which his travels have brought him of almost every part of the Empire. Thus it also happens that, at a time when the Crown has come to play a new and predominant part in the political unity of the Empire, its wearer is, thanks to his own indomitable energy and to his father's foresight, known " in his proper person " to an unprecedented number of his subjects. " We saw the Prince " has been the delighted claim of hundreds of thousands of oversea citizens in past years, not in the great cities alone, but in the back blocks too. " We know the King " will be their no less proud boast to-day. Nor is it the knowledge of passing acquaintance that may end with a handshake or a wave in the streets. The King, as Britain and the Dominions have reason to know, is a

47

personality, and his doings have been followed with that close and affectionate interest which testifies not only to his eminence and ubiquity as a public figure but to the interest of his character and the appeal of his qualities. They could hardly fail to command the popular confidence and honest liking with which, in full store, he begins his reign. Among the cardinal virtues courage may perhaps be sure of the widest allegiance. There is no question that the King shares to the fullest extent in the physical courage that has always been among the endowments of his House. Equally characteristic of him, as of his father and grandfather, is his utter freedom from all trace of affectation and pretentiousness, his unerring eye for the distinction between dignity and solemnity. No man is more willing to make friends, and none has a greater regard for the obligations of friendship. At the same time he values humanity in the widest sense of the old aphorism. Men, not books, are his library, as they were for the last King Edward, and he has the same power to learn from them. He is gifted with a genuine interest, which more " democrats " profess than feel, in all sorts and conditions of people, and he is rich in a study that is admirable and endearing in any man and inestimable in a Sovereign—the study of mankind.

Such is the personality which has put so remarkable a spell upon the imagination of the many communities within what is henceforth his realm, and indeed of many beyond its borders. And in the heart of it is that vitality which can neither be acquired nor invented and is the master-key to other hearts. As every one of his contemporaries knows, it has irradiated the great service which he has done the Commonwealth during his years as Heir to the Throne, in Empire countries, in foreign lands, and in the wide industrial areas of our own island. It is as recognizable in his zest for new experience and in the versatility which has followed from it. It is attested in his most secular tastes. The undergraduate who could hardly be induced to mount a horse soon became the devotee of hunting and steeplechasing. When circumstances forbade the thrills of horsemanship in its more perilous forms he turned to flying. As pilot and passenger he has shown himself a true participator in the modern mind, especially in the help he has given to the progress of air transport generally by treating a venturous novelty as one of the common-places of locomotion. For other recreation he turned to golf and was not long in wresting from that disciplinary game a marked degree of proficiency ; and now gardening, with its own claims upon patience and specialization, has come in turn to share with golf the interests of his leisure. These may seem smaller examples than they truly are in the context of great responsibilities and of the interests of the State. They belong very intimately to the man they describe, and they tell truthfully of his eagerness for life and its variety, of a versatility that is not necessarily fickleness, of a vitality that, in small things and great, is deceived by no illusion of effortless success.

The broad views distinctive of the new King are deeply rooted in a broad education. In early youth he learnt discipline and thoroughness from the Navy. Oxford gave him the freedom of living among, and learning from, men of his own age and the varied guidance of such teachers as Sir Herbert Warren, the President of his own college, Sir William Anson, and Sir Charles Grant Robertson. The War carried him thence to a sterner training-ground, one that was fruitful again in all that may be learnt in the encounters of a free and ever-changing society, judging every man on his merits as he responded to the most rigorous of all tests, fruitful too in the greatest lesson of all—the power of a fellowship existing for aims that lay even beyond self-preservation and victory. There, as the young man of twenty-four could truly say, " I found my manhood." And then, after the microcosm of Oxford and the world of the Army, the world itself. To read again the tale of the journeys of the Prince of Wales between 1919 and 1931 is almost to doubt its truth. India and every Dominion visited, South Africa twice and Canada thrice, and many of the Colonies ; a journey to Japan ; two separate journeys to the United States ; and two to Latin America. The bare summary is eloquence itself. Wherever the Prince went he left behind him a rich legacy of good will and understanding, and brought away with him knowledge by which he, his advisers, and his Empire cannot fail to profit in the coming years. Nor have his travels ended there. Not less importantly, they have carried him from end to end of this island. He knows at first hand, and by thousands of individual samplings, who and what the people of Britain are. He knows them in their work and play, and he knows in particular how and under what conditions they win their livelihood. No one who has heard him speak on the subject of employment and unemployment can doubt the passionate earnestness with which his mind is put to it. Just in

H

the same spirit as he learnt Spanish before his last South American visit, so he has fitted himself by personal study and by continuous consultation with experts to take the fullest part open to him in bettering the "condition of the people."

Under good augury, then, and with high hope, the nation offers its homage and pledges its loyalty to King Edward VIII. Four years younger than his father was at the time of his accession, he comes to the Throne at a time which gives some sinister promise of resemblance to events in the first years of the late reign and much happy certainty of divergence from them. Then, as now, there was lacking, perhaps more ominously, a settled prospect of stability in international relations. At home it is otherwise. Never has our policy been more united, fundamentally, in its conception and pursuit of national needs abroad and at home. While it would be presumptuous to attempt a forecast of the contribution which His Majesty may feel specially qualified to make towards those needs, it will no doubt be guided by his well-known admiration for the work of his grandfather as the ambassador of peace and friendship between the nations of Europe. Just as King Edward VII strove, and strove successfully, to interpret Britain to France and France to Britain, so his own exceptional experience of the English-speaking countries, the Dominions and the United States, might seem to invite King Edward VIII to the mission of strengthening the links between them. Whether this be so or not, and whatever the distinguishing marks of the new reign may prove to be, every part of the Empire is one in the conviction that the King—and, as India will warmly claim, the King-Emperor—will be heart and soul with every true effort for the greater happiness and security of his Dominions and for the promotion of the world's peace. In the life of responsibility, day in and day out, which will henceforth be his, he will lack the help and counsel of a consort. While all his brothers have made happy marriages, the new King ascends the Throne a bachelor. But it will be his fortune to be able to turn to the wisdom and experience of the gracious lady whose devoted part in the great story of the past twenty-five years is known to all and was the subject of a memorable passage in one of King George's Jubilee speeches. With gratitude unquenchable for the father's life and work, with confidence high in the promise of the son, the nation sets its face forward again. The prayer of yesterday is echoed in the benediction of to-day. God Save the King.

CHAPTER III

FROM SANDRINGHAM TO WESTMINSTER HALL

O N January 23 the body of King George was brought from the parish church at Sandringham to lie in state in Westminster Hall. The first stage of this, King George's last journey, was carried out in the presence of an astonishing concourse—astonishing in a corner of England so thinly populated. Outside the gates leading from the parish church was an extemporized car park in which were some thousands of motor-cars, and this was but one of several. Parties of children came from neighbouring villages in haywains.

Yet it was a simple, even an intimate leave-taking. Though what ceremony there was was beautifully ordered, the prevalent feeling was almost wholly personal. Unaffected sorrow at the loss of a kind master and friend, the country gentleman in whom King George perhaps most loved to merge his sovereignty ; unobtrusive sympathy for the Royal widow and her children in their wholly human grief : these emotions could here be given expression single-heartedly. To so many of those who walked behind the coffin or watched it pass, King George was firstly their squire and employer on the Sandringham estate. An old pensioner, a man who worked there for about fifty years, stood outside the gates that morning. He was invited inside the park, with the other tenants, but he felt, he said, too much upset to join them there. He was all but crying. " I worked for his father," he said. " When he was a little boy "—this was King George—" he used to play with my rakes, him and the Duke o' Clarence. They often hid 'em in the bushes and then laughed when I couldn't find 'em."

The natural setting of the route to Wolferton had a heart-easing beauty that January day. It was a very gracious morning, notwithstanding the frost which, till the mounting sun brushed it away, added white tips to the grass and the moss on the old wall round Sandringham. Every one who was there must in years to come be glad to remember that on such a morning King George's beloved Sandringham said good-bye to him. The sky was unclouded blue ; the strong, steady sunshine was like a calm benediction.

The King, his three brothers, and Lord Harewood walked to the church from Sandringham House by the most direct path. Queen Mary, with the Royal ladies, all heavily veiled, drove there by way of the old Norwich Gates in two carriages. The men waiting outside the ivy-crowned lych-gate all bared their heads as the Royal mourners arrived and entered. The King and Queen Mary sat beside each other in the pew on the south side of the chancel. The service was conducted by the Bishop of Norwich and the rector, the Rev. A. R. Fuller. The choir boys sang the 23rd Psalm; the one hymn was "Peace, perfect peace." The simple service was soon over. Then Grenadier Guardsmen, bareheaded, lifted the coffin and carried it out and down the steps to the gun-carriage. The King fell in just behind the coffin, and behind him his brothers and Lord Harewood. Queen Mary entered the first carriage with the Princess Royal and the Duchess of York. In the second carriage were the Duchess of Gloucester, the Duchess of Kent, and the Queen's two ladies-in-waiting, Lady Desborough and Lady Elizabeth Motion.

From the cross-roads outside the gates there was heard very faintly wailing music from the bagpipes of the King's Piper. It was the first and the only music that reached any ear beyond the park. A minute later came the procession. In front walked the Chief Constable of Norfolk between two other police officers of high rank. Next came the Guards. Grey greatcoats hid their scarlet, and they were unarmed except for the bayonets in their white belts. They came forward at a quick march, the pace of the whole procession. A mounted officer of the Royal Horse Artillery in plumed busby and with drawn sword preceded the gun-carriage. Like the drivers of the six bay horses of the gun team, he wore his greatcoat of khaki. Draped over the coffin was the Royal Standard, and on it were two simple wreaths from Queen Mary and her family, nothing more. For all the richness of the covering it looked a very simple coffin for a King.

King Edward walked, pale and with set features, alone. His three brothers and his brother-in-law were side by side. Each of them wore a black overcoat and was carrying his silk hat. The

The Lying-in-State in Westminster Hall.

Royal ladies could be seen dimly in their closed carriages. Two grey horses drew the carriage of Queen Mary, a pair of bays the second carriage. The drivers wore silk hats and drab overcoats. Then, most touching in its symbolism, came a saddled grey pony, its whiteness almost dazzling in sudden contrast with the sombre tones before and after. This was King George's pretty shooting pony, Jock. The old pensioner at the cross-roads, when he saw Jock, said, " I passed him, riding his pony, one day last week. The Queen was walking at his side." There came behind high officers of the Royal Household-in-waiting, led by Lord Wigram, Keeper of the Privy Purse and Private Secretary to King George, and Lord Claud Hamilton, Equerry to the King. A great company followed on foot. There were hundreds of plainly-dressed tenants and servants on the estate, besides mayoral delegations from neighbouring towns and other local authorities, including one mayor in furred robes and many mace-bearers. The King's Piper walked with the rest, in front of a group of woodmen in dark green brass-buttoned coats and bowler hats.

From the north side of the railway came the sound of marching men. Over the level-crossing and into the enclosed station approach at Wolferton passed the Sandringham Company of the 5th Battalion, The Norfolk Regiment, Territorial Army, with draped Colour and muffled drums, at present silent. The men lined up to form a guard of honour, while outside the station gates and for some distance along the roadway stood a single file of 100 members of the British Legion, with draped standards of blue and gold. They represented a large number of the eighty Norfolk branches of the Legion and included two survivors of the War-time Sandringham Company of The Norfolk Regiment.

A roll of muffled drums at 10 minutes to 12 told of the approach of the procession. Presently on the brow of the hill its head came into view. The men of the Legion bared their heads and came to attention. As the gun-carriage slowly passed standards were dipped at the salute, and from the Royal approach to the station came the music of Chopin's Funeral March. King Edward turned his head as if expressing gratitude for the ex-Service men's salute to his dead father. The coffin was borne to the train through the red-carpeted vestibule of the Royal entrance. Flowers were quickly transferred from a motor-van to the train.

The band again played Chopin's Funeral March, and at five minutes past noon the train glided slowly and almost silently from the station.

Along the railway were lines of people who had come out to make their last tributes of respect as the funeral train passed. In the towns windows and even roofs near the railway were crowded with bareheaded onlookers. In the countryside there were groups on the field paths and along the fences. At level crossings halted motor-cars stretched out in solid columns on either hand and their occupants had spread themselves out over the fields adjoining the line. At King's Lynn, as the train passed the edge of the playing fields of King Edward VII Grammar School, the 400 boys and their masters stood caps in hand beside the railway track. Elsewhere there were organized parties of schoolchildren as well as adults, and finally, as the train made its way into London, it passed between continuous lines of people bent upon paying their mute tokens of homage.

The Royal train reached King's Cross, London, at a quarter to 3. It came into a silent station, where traffic was still and the hiss of steam had been hushed. Its own arrival made no sound. Its steam added nothing to the faint mistiness in the station. For all the red carpet and purple drapings the bare station could have no beauty, but it had an air of sombre reverence and quiet dignity as the mortal remains of the King came to the end of their longest journey.

In the darkened roadway beside the platform the Guards of Honour from the Navy, the Grenadier Guards, and the Royal Air Force had already brought their rifles with fixed bayonets to the " present " and stood rigid. A few black-coated officials waited on the platform. The gun-carriage, with its six horses, was ready to move forward to the place where it might receive its Royal burden. The double doors of the saloon in which the body of King George lay were gently opened. The door of Queen Mary's saloon, next behind it, was opened. No sound yet broke the stillness.

For a moment the train was as still as the place was silent. Then King Edward descended from his saloon and moved to the door of Queen Mary's coach to assist his mother and then his sister to alight. The Royal Dukes and their ladies followed. Led by the King and Queen Mary, the little black-garbed party

54

moved forward towards the open doors of the funeral coach. There at the edge of the red carpet, which had silenced their foot-steps too, the mourners halted, the Queen in a long black coat and long enveloping veil, with the King, bareheaded, on one side of her, and the Princess Royal, similarly veiled, on the other. The King and the Duke of York went quietly forward to the door of the coach while the coffin was being shrouded in the Royal Standard. Then the Imperial Crown, covered with a purple cloth, was carried into the coach and was placed on the coffin.

Meanwhile the gun-carriage had been driven up without a clink of harness or the noticeable rumble of wheels on the sanded roadway. It drew up, and, while it waited, the King, with the Princess Royal, entered the funeral coach, the Princess to place Queen Mary's cross of white flowers at the head of the coffin, the King to satisfy himself personally that his father's coffin was properly arrayed for its passage through the streets to Westminster. These small filial duties completed, the King and his sister rejoined Queen Mary, and Guards and officials stood motionless, as before, for orders which would allow them to take the coffin from the train.

The little procession might now have moved off in decorous progress ten minutes before its appointed time. Her Majesty was consulted by the King, and her decision evidently was to wait quietly on the platform for the official hour of departure. The King, acquiescing, at once thought of the guards of honour standing motionless at the " present " the width of the road away. He went himself to the officer in charge of the gun-carriage and made known the wish of himself and Queen Mary. A few moments elapsed and then in succession the words of command rang out. Rifles were brought down to the " order " and the men were stood at ease. The hush which had received the dead King had been unbroken until his coffin was ready to go on its path of public mourning.

The three guards of honour became still again. The Royal party stood in two rows on the platform facing the path by which the body must be borne to the gun-carriage. For six minutes more the great building and its gloomy arches were emptied of sound and movement. The scene gave a sense of the parting of the ways, as though the little family group had paused before merging its private grief in the great tide of public sorrow

55

waiting to manifest itself in the crowded streets. Here in the unlighted vault of an empty railway station the last act of affection and respect was passing to the husband and the father, before the people of a King should claim the privilege of paying him its own tribute.

Four minutes before 3 o'clock the King nodded his permission to the officials for the ceremony of removal to proceed. The eight Guardsmen bearers began to emerge with their Royal burden from the funeral coach. The sailors and soldiers presented arms once more to the King they had served. The coffin, wholly covered by its Standard, began its slow progress on the level shoulders of its bearers across the sanded path on the platform, passing close to the King and Queen Mary. Gently it was placed on the gun-carriage. Smoothly it was slid along the rollers, the Crown and the white cross undisturbed. The fringes of the Royal Standard were drawn clear of the wheels. The King took his position immediately behind the gun-carriage. The Duke of York and the Duke of Gloucester fell in behind him, and behind them again were the Duke of Kent and the Earl of Harewood.

At once the small procession moved away. Queen Mary and the ladies of the Royal Family stood until it had passed. Then a car drew alongside. Queen Mary and the Princess Royal entered, and at the Queen's invitation the Duchess of York, the Duchess of Gloucester, and the Duchess of Kent joined them in the same car.

From King's Cross to Westminster Hall, by way of Euston Road, Southampton Row, Kingsway, the Strand, and Whitehall, the body of the dead King on its gun-carriage passed between dense masses of people standing silently on either side of the roadway and many proving unable to control their grief. Some of the people had been there for hours, and almost all wore some sign of mourning. The route was kept by thousands of police and special constables, who had little to do in controlling a crowd whose one desire was to be quiet and orderly. Military display there was none, save for the guards of honour at the station and Westminster Hall and the funeral procession itself.

This was pathetic and moving in its brief simplicity, the simplest display, perhaps, with which King George ever passed on a state occasion through the streets of his capital. Five policemen on white horses in front and four behind were the only escort. The team of the Royal Horse Artillery, in their dark overcoats, were only relieved in colour by a few gleams of gold, their white plumes, and the scarlet of their busby bags. The coffin lay on the gun-carriage under the Royal Standard, and on it glittered the Imperial Crown and a beautiful cross of flowers. Beside it in their overcoats marched the bearer party of the Grenadier Guards.

Behind slowly walked King Edward in deep mourning with his head bowed, the light gleaming on his fair hair, and his face stern with grief. On either side of him were his brothers, the Dukes of York and Gloucester, and then came the Duke of Kent and the Earl of Harewood. A score or so of bare-headed members of the late King's household completed the procession.

Meantime there were those who awaited in Westminster Hall the last coming of the King. Those who, a short six months ago, saw the gracious gesture and heard the resonant tones with which he returned thanks in that noble building for the congratulations of Parliament on his Jubilee could hardly believe that the active, smiling figure of their memory was no more. The very building seemed to mourn in the chill, cold light of the wintry afternoon. The gay dais and stands of the days of Jubilee were gone, and in their place stood the sombre catafalque, a squat pedestal draped in purple with a golden border standing on a square of purple-draped steps. The rows of seats, filled with a joyous and exultant audience, had given place to a vast emptiness, in which, during the time of waiting, a few groups of dark figures stood or strolled. And in place of the summer sun, which at Jubilee time turned the great window into a blazing jewel and the mighty rafters into a delicate oaken tracery, four huge candles at the corners of the catafalque and two clusters of electric light alone relieved a deep and somehow humid gloom.

From time to time a group in deepest mourning, one of them including the Duchesses of York, Gloucester, and Kent, entered and took their places on the great flight of steps beneath the window, until the steps themselves seemed to be draped in black. A few officers, some in the long cloaks and towering plumes of the Gentlemen at Arms, others in brilliant scarlet, stood on either side of the catafalque. A company of the Yeomen of the Guard busied themselves with final preparations for the night's vigil. The rest was oppressive silence and expectation.

The first sign of ceremony was the appearance of the three Kings of Arms with Pursuivants and Heralds, whose dress was the quartered arms of the United Kingdom. They passed down the length of the hall and took station near the main door. Shortly afterwards the Lord Chancellor appeared, leading the Peers, who passed slowly down the steps and ranged themselves on the right of the hall.

Lord Hailsham himself stood with the officers of the House of Lords in the centre. On his right were the Bishops, and the Lords Temporal extended the whole length of the hall, so many had come to do the dead King honour. Five minutes later the Speaker, in the special robes of black and gold reserved for State occasions, entered at the head of the Commons, who lined the side of the hall opposite to the Lords. Then on the top of the steps appeared the Archbishop of Canterbury, followed by the Dean of Westminster and the choir of the Chapel Royal, and preceded by a tall golden cross. The choir took station on the steps, where their white surplices chequered the black of the waiting mourners. The Archbishop and the Dean passed down to the door, where they joined the Earl Marshal and the First Commissioner of Works and prepared to meet the *cortège*.

A slight haze had replaced the clear sky of the early afternoon as the procession from King's Cross passed into Parliament Square and through the gates of New Palace Yard to Westminster Hall. To the mourners who had walked through the crowded streets, and nowhere was there a greater gathering than outside New Palace Yard, it must have been like entering a haven of peace and rest. Occupation of the yard was confined to Guards of Honour of the three Services, who presented arms and lowered their Colours. The arrival at Westminster Hall was another example of the triumph of organization so frequently recorded on great occasions in this country. The procession was timed to reach Westminster Hall at 4 o'clock, and it was as Big Ben boomed out the first stroke of the hour that the gun-carriage came to a halt at the entrance.

Under the canopy which had been erected outside Westminster Hall the Archbishop of Canterbury, the Lord Great Chamberlain, the Earl Marshal, and the First Commissioner of Works stood waiting while the bearer party reverently raised the coffin. Waiting also was Queen Mary, who had arrived by motor-car a few minutes previously. As with slow steps the bearer party carried the coffin into Westminster Hall the Union Jack flying

The coffin being brought out from Westminster Hall.

A section of the crowds in Parliament Street.

at half-mast on the Victoria Tower fluttered down and the Royal Standard was hoisted in its place. Once more a King had come to Westminster to lie in state.

The procession to the waiting catafalque was :

Pursuivants.
Heralds.

Norroy King of Arms.		Clarenceux King of Arms.
Black Rod.	The First Commissioner of Works.	Garter.
The Earl Marshal.		The Lord Great Chamberlain.

The Dean of Westminster.
The Archbishop of Canterbury.

His Majesty THE KING.		Her Majesty QUEEN MARY.
His Royal Highness The Duke of Gloucester.	Her Royal Highness The Princess Royal.	His Royal Highness The Duke of York.
The Earl of Harewood.	His Royal Highness The Duke of Kent.	

In dead silence the procession advanced. The bearers slid the coffin on to the catafalque, stood a minute at attention, and marched forward and away. The mourners halted ; and the Archbishop, turning round, read a few simple prayers. There was a hush ; then, from the steps the choir broke into the solemn but exultant hymn " Praise, my soul, the King of heaven." As the echoes of the last note died away the Archbishop pronounced the Benediction, and all hearts echoed its final message to the living and to the dead : " The Lord lift up the light of His countenance upon thee and give thee peace, now and for evermore."

It was over. The Royal mourners turned and passed out. Lords and Commons passed two abreast down the Hall, back past the catafalque, and out by the way they had come. There were left only four Yeomen standing with bowed heads at the four corners and the few officers charged with special duties. Silence, solitude, and peace stood about the dead King.

The scene at night was symbolical both of the glory which King George earned as King and the affection which he inspired as a man. Lit only by four clusters of lights hanging from the roof, the catafalque had something of the outstanding dignity possessed by the Cenotaph, which commemorates those who died in the service of His Majesty. The standard which draped the coffin was turned into a richly coloured canopy, and the jewelled Crown glowed and sparkled. Two more great candles, making six in all, had been added at the head and feet.

The guard of four Yeomen, leaning on their long halberds, was still there, but an inner guard had joined them. At the head of the coffin, on the lowest of the three steps of the catafalque, stood four gigantic Gentlemen-at-Arms in long dark blue cloaks, with the white plumes of their helmets drooped in alignment. At each corner of the main platform stood a Lifeguardsman in plumed helmet, scarlet tunic with mourning band on the left arm, white breeches and high black boots. Their hands, in white gauntlets, were crossed upon the hilt of their swords, whose points rested on the ground.

Readers of the story " In the Presence " by that other great Englishman who was laid to rest so recently will remember the strain of this sentinelship. But, as in Kipling's story round the coffin of King Edward VII, so now round the coffin of King George V these sentinels stood motionless, the very embodiment of a nation's mourning. Only when the guard was changed did they turn from statues into men.

The reliefs advanced in single file from the guardroom above the staircase on the right of the hall, separated, and mounted each to a corner, where they stood beside the still motionless sentinel. All as one man drew their swords, placed the tips on the ground with one hand and swung out the other arm straight from the shoulder. In a single action this outflung hand was brought back to the sword-hilt and the head dropped on the chest. At the same instant the heads of the former sentinels were raised erect, their swords were brought up to the carry, they stepped slowly off the platform, formed up, and paced away.

Thus, solemnly guarded, the dead King waited to grant the last audience to his people. They came in their hundreds and in their thousands and in their hundreds of thousands. For four days the last audience continued, and it seemed as if the procession of subjects—they numbered in all nearly 800,000—would never end. On the first day, January 24, the queue at times was a mile long, and during the day alone 110,000 entered Westminster Hall. In the evening King Edward and Queen Mary were present and remained for ten minutes, the hall for the time being emptied of the public. They were accompanied by other members of the Royal Family and by the King and Queen of Norway, who had arrived in London that day for the funeral.

Through an amazing week-end the procession continued. It was rare to see a mourner whose raiment did not bear some mourning sign. All sorts and conditions of men and women were there, the very old, the very young, the infirm, the ailing.

Entering the south door of the hall, the procession divided into two files and passed down the stone steps and along either side of the hall, passing out by the entrance into Palace Yard. The people moved through the hall two or three abreast, walking slowly but never lingering, except when the policemen on duty halted the procession for a few moments to allow for the relieving of the guards around the catafalque. To pass thus through Westminster Hall occupied between two and three minutes, but it was long enough for those who went by to pay their final tribute to King George and to carry away an impression of the scene unlikely soon to fade.

At one time the queue extended not merely to Vauxhall Bridge, but over it and along the east bank of the Thames. All classes and all callings among King George's subjects seemed to have their representatives in the long procession.

Some lingered for a moment when they entered at the head of the flight of stone steps, gazing far down the hall at the lighted catafalque and the motionless figures of the surrounding guards, at the draped coffin with the Imperial Crown resting amid the folds of the Royal Standard, and at the golden cross which surmounted the whole. At the same time the two long lines of people were to be seen moving slowly down the hall on either side, and at intervals, from the double flight of stone steps on the left, the brilliantly clad forms of the relieving guards came with a slow and silent tread to move almost imperceptibly into their places around the bier. The lieutenant-colonels commanding the five regiments of the Brigade of Guards took their share in the service of loyal vigil by the bier when they performed the

61

midday watch. Among others who kept guard over the bier was Captain Sir Beachcroft Towse, the blind V.C., one of the Gentlemen-at-Arms.

By 4 o'clock on the first day of the lying-in-state the gloom of evening was deepening the heavy shadows in the hall, and the Yeomen of the Guard were relieved by four other Yeomen wearing blue cloaks with crimson-lined hoods. The scarlet uniforms of the Gentlemen-at-Arms also gave place to blue greatcoats. But in spite of the chilliness of the great hall the officers of the Guards who stood one at each corner of the catafalque continued their vigil in the dress worn throughout the day and their scarlet tunics shone out vividly. About this time the illumination of the magnificent oak roof was increased and in bay after bay the carved shields and angels and the massive rafters were gloriously bathed in a glow of light. Those who passed the King's bier after nightfall saw the naked beauty of the hall of William Rufus at its best.

A lasting impression of the scene in the hall was the silence with which thousands of people were reverently passing by the bier. On the strips of grey carpet which had been laid down their footfalls made no sound, and it was odd during the slow passage of this mighty pilgrimage to note how sharply the silence would be broken by the cry of an infant carried in its mother's arms or by the occasional sound of a motor-horn in the streets outside. The only other sound to be heard was the measured tread of the Gentlemen-at-Arms as they walked up the middle of the stone floor to and from St. Stephen's Hall for the changing of their guard, their plumes towering above the crowds which parted to make way for their stately progress.

It was one of the Gentlemen-at-Arms—all of them elderly officers of distinction—who was overcome by the ordeal of the vigil on Thursday night, January 23. According to witnesses of the occurrence this officer displayed self-control to a marked degree. While standing with the three other Gentlemen-at-Arms on guard at the foot of the coffin he apparently felt himself being overcome by faintness. He slowly stepped from the rank, turned about, and at the same solemn pace as that at which he had arrived to watch over his dead Sovereign he marched along the hall and up the great flight of steps to St. Stephen's Porch. Those who saw him pass did not realize that he was ill.

As soon as he had passed the doors into St. Stephen's Hall the Gentleman-at-Arms collapsed. His place at the coffin was immediately taken by one of his brother officers.

Of the hundreds of thousands who made the pilgrimage many were there three hours or more on the Saturday before what had been the procession's tail when they arrived became its head. This evolutionary process and these unexampled scenes continued without intermission from 8 a.m. to a little after midnight on that day. In that time 150,770 people were officially reckoned to have passed through Westminster Hall. On the Friday most of the pilgrims had to wait in drizzling rain; those who followed them on the Saturday morning endured a peculiarly discomforting blend of rain and fog. The half-masted flags overhead drooped from a sad sky, a mourning sky. If the multitude with its umbrellas and wraps and overcoats did not compose romantically there was yet a suggestion of nobility in the drab picture. At 9.30 p.m., half an hour before the hall should have been closed for the night, the end of the procession still reached almost to the Tate Gallery and it still numbered perhaps 20,000 souls. Mounted and foot policemen then formed a moving barrier behind the last comers, and all those between this barrier and St. Stephen's Porch were allowed to enter.

After the experience of this second day of the lying-in-state it was at once decided not to close the hall on the third occasion till 1 o'clock in the morning. That decision was reconsidered, and it was then announced that Westminster Hall would remain open till 6 a.m., two hours before the final day's pilgrimage would officially begin. At the time when this decision was reached the procession extended as far as St. Thomas's Hospital, and it was taking seven hours or more to cover the distance to Westminster Hall along both banks of the river. Traffic arrangements had naturally by that time gone to pieces. Some hours earlier notices had been posted at Underground stations warning the people to travel to Victoria rather than Westminster on their way to join the procession.

Sunday, the 26th, was pleasantly fine by comparison with Saturday, after a rainy night. A few people, equipped with camp stools, had been waiting outside Westminster Hall since soon after the last of Saturday's throng had gone away. By 5 a.m. there was a queue numbering some hundreds. Those who arrived at 8 o'clock, when the hall was reopened, fell in on the pavement a little beyond Lambeth Bridge. For them the time of waiting was rather more than an hour before they found themselves at the top of the broad steps leading down into Westminster Hall. In the first hour, between 8 and 9 a.m., about 15,000 people passed through the hall, compared with an average of under 10,000 an hour on the previous day. Every effort was made by the hundreds of forbearing police who marshalled the crowds to maintain this quickened rate of progress, and with conspicuous success in the earlier part of the day.

As the hours passed the numbers increased, until by the early evening the back of the close-packed queue was on the embankment on the riverside front of St. Thomas's Hospital, near Westminster Bridge. Those who wished to join it had to go down the steps from the bridge, and for this purpose three streams of people moved continuously, up Westminster Bridge Road from Lambeth ; up Stangate and Lambeth Palace Road from Vauxhall ; and over the bridge from Westminster.

Wheeled traffic was barred by the police from Lambeth Bridge, though it was open to pedestrians who were outside the queue, and this much accelerated the progress of the waiting people across each end of the bridge. The length of the queue at this time was calculated to be between two-and-a-half and three miles.

A police car with a loud-speaker on the roof travelled slowly up and down with an officer at intervals directing the new arrivals to the end of the queue, and informing them that the hall would be open till 6 o'clock in the morning. In Abingdon Street and Millbank, from Parliament Square, there were, however, still many walking southward towards Vauxhall Bridge, unaware that the end of the queue was just over Westminster Bridge.

Between 11 o'clock and midnight 17,049 persons passed the catafalque, making a total of 251,166 during the day and over half a million since the lying-in-state began.

At midnight there was still a long queue, but it ended on the Millbank end of Vauxhall Bridge and was steadily dwindling in length.

Before the doors were opened on the Saturday morning Queen Mary sent a fresh cross of beautiful flowers, white and pink, to

Some of the representatives of the Dominions in the funeral procession. They
include the Raja of Sawantwadi and the Maharajah of Dhrangadhra, Mr. S. M.
Bruce, Mr. Vincent Massey, Mr. C. te Water .and Sir James Parr.

M. Litvinoff, M. le Breton, Baron von Neurath, and other representatives of
foreign Powers in the funeral procession.

be laid on the coffin beside the Crown, orb, and sceptre, in place of the flowers which had previously rested there. Early in the evening of the same day the Duke and Duchess of Kent entered the hall by the Members' Entrance and stood for a short time watching the mourners pass. At 10 p.m. the hall was closed to the public for a few minutes to allow representatives of foreign Embassies and Legations, High Commissioners for the Dominions, foreign delegates to the Naval Conference, and other distinguished visitors to pass through the hall. Prince Starhemberg of Austria was one of them.

The Princess Royal and the Earl of Harewood brought their two sons from Buckingham Palace, and with them were Princess Louise, Duchess of Argyll, and Princess Helena Victoria. The Infanta Beatrice, daughter of the ex-King of Spain, and the King of Bulgaria also went to the hall. Mr. Baldwin also spent some time by the catafalque.

The composition of the crowd changed and changed again, the light in the hall varied from morning to noon from noon to dusk and night ; but all that changed in the rich centrepiece was the dress of the dozen watchers round King George's body. The four Gentlemen-at-Arms in line at one end, and the four Yeomen of the Guard who stood, one at each corner, on the lowest purple-draped step of the pedestal, were clad through the chill nights and early mornings in dark blue cloaks that hid most of their bright scarlet. The four officers whose posts were at the corners of the topmost tier wore no greatcoats at any time ; but the regiments represented, and therefore the uniforms, changed every six hours. Thus the passing hours brought their own contributions of light and colour to a scene sublime and arresting in its majesty.

The military watchers and the Gentlemen-at-Arms were relieved every twenty minutes, the Yeomen of the Guard each hour. At longer intervals officials came into the hall with a pair of steps and snuffed the tall candles—tall enough to burn for seventy-two hours. In the night, when the doors were closed, even though the stately and rigid ceremonial round the catafalque went on always, cleaners entered the hall and swept the carpets which the scores of thousands of feet had trod all day. In a railed-off corner doctors and nurses from Westminster Hospital took duty in relays, though only trifling cases required their attention.

F

Nurses from this and the other hospitals were admitted to see the lying-in-state by a corner entrance, since their free hours were few.

The day's pilgrimage which had begun at 8 a.m. on the Sunday did not end until 3.40 a.m. on the Monday, the hall having been closed at that hour and not at 6 as announced. After an interval of only three hours and a half the hall was reopened and the vast procession began anew. People had begun to assemble before half-past 4.

Queen Mary sent fresh flowers, a cross of lilies, white carnations and chrysanthemums. By half-past 9 in dismal rain the queue was already beyond Lambeth Bridge, and by noon stretched right across Vauxhall Bridge. The rain stopped, and the queue, which had slightly diminished, grew again. Prince and Princess Arthur of Connaught were present when a contingent of nurses from the Middlesex Hospital arrived. After watching the impressive ceremony of the changing of the guard around the catafalque at 3 o'clock, they slipped all but unnoticed into the general procession and passed the coffin of King George with the rest of his people. Later in the afternoon King Carol of Rumania, accompanied by the Duke of York, visited the hall. Shortly afterwards Prince Frederick of Prussia came.

A few minutes before the change of guard at 6 o'clock five motor-cars drove into New Palace Yard and through the archway to the private entrance to Westminster Hall. In the first, which bore the Royal Arms, was Queen Mary, heavily veiled, accompanied by Princess Elizabeth. The time of the visit was especially arranged by the Queen. She desired that Princess Elizabeth should see for herself not only the magnificence of the catafalque in its perfect setting, but also the dignified ceremony with which the guard was changed.

In the following cars came the King and Queen of Norway, Prince Olaf of Norway, the King of Denmark, the King of the Belgians, the Crown Prince of Italy, Prince Axel of Denmark, the Duke and Duchess of York, the Duke and Duchess of Gloucester, the Duke of Kent, the Comte de Flandres, Prince Ernest Augustus of Hanover, Prince Frederick of Prussia, the Princess Royal and the Earl of Harewood, Prince George of Greece and Prince Nicholas of Greece. At the entrance to the hall they were received by the First Commissioner of Works.

The Queen and those who were with her entered by the door-way in the middle of the eastern side of the hall, which brought them immediately opposite King George's bier. The Royal party came in so unobtrusively that many then inside the hall did not realize that they were present. For a few minutes the file of those moving down the right-hand side of the hall was stopped, but on the left-hand side the people still moved forward.

Almost as soon as the Royal party had entered, the guard around the catafalque was changed, and the Queen and the other mourners moved forward to watch the ceremony. From the double flight of descending steps against the opposite wall, officers of the 1st Battalion of the Grenadier Guards, wearing bands of black crêpe on the sleeves of their scarlet tunics, came with slow and measured paces to replace their brother officers of the Horse Guards. When the ceremony was over, the Royal party moved back into the open space near the wall, and again the file of people advanced down the hall. The Queen and her companions did not leave for some time longer, but remained standing near the entrance by which they had come, watching the lighted bier and the unbroken lines of people moving past it. The eyes of all were upon the catafalque, and few heads were turned towards the Royal watchers of the scene. The Queen was unrecognized by many people there.

At 10.30 the queue was still halfway across Vauxhall Bridge, and by midnight another 15,350 people had passed through the hall ; the muffled tread of myriad feet went on and there came unexpected, unheralded and realized by few another act in this vast drama of homage and majesty. Shortly after midnight the King and his three brothers took part in the mounting of the guard over the dead King at the catafalque. The customary changing of the guard had taken place when an officer, approaching the catafalque, saluted the Colour lying on the catafalque and removed it. Almost immediately afterwards the King, in the uniform of the Welsh Guards, marched from the entrance of the Guards' officers' quarters to the catafalque. With him were the Duke of York, in the uniform of the Scots Guards, the Duke of Gloucester, in the uniform of the 10th Hussars, and the Duke of Kent, in naval uniform.

They took up position in between the Guards already on duty, the King facing the steps of St. Stephen's, with the Duke of

Kent on his right, the Duke of Gloucester on his left, and the Duke of York facing Palace Yard. They remained motionless, resting on their swords, for about a quarter of an hour, and then they slowly moved away from the catafalque and marched back to the Guards' quarters.

LEADING ARTICLES FROM "THE TIMES"

SQUIRE AND KING

ON Tuesday afternoon, as twilight was beginning to fall, a coffin made from oak grown on the place was carried out of the door of a country house in Norfolk and laid upon a hand-bier. The bearers were woodmen and gamekeepers. The lament played by a piper told of Scottish affinities in the family ; and the party of Grenadier Guards, walking beside the bier as escort from the house to the parish church in the park, showed that the dead man was an officer of that regiment. Arrived at the church, the coffin was carried inside by Grenadiers, and laid upon a bier before the altar ; and there it was watched, night and day, by woodmen, gardeners, and other servants of the estate, four at a time, until yesterday morning. During Wednesday tenants and others of the neighbourhood came to pay their last respects. Yesterday morning the coffin was put upon a gun-carriage, and at a walking pace, followed on foot by the heir and his brothers and a train of members of the household, villagers, and tenants, it was taken some two and a half miles along a country road, lined by local police, to a railway station, where it was awaited by a detachment of the local Territorials.

In all this there is nothing to indicate that the dead man thus honoured was greater than a country gentleman and landowner. Leaving home for the last time, King George left it in the character in which he had lived there—the " squire " of Sandringham, the master and friend of scores of the workers and dwellers in rural England, men, women, and children whose work and whose lives were known to him, and whose welfare he made, so far as possible, his personal care. Not so adventurously and so far afield as his heir, but seriously and practically, King George was a farmer. His life at Sandringham was the life of a country gentleman, among his own people, who saw in him the squire first, the King second. So it was also at Balmoral. He was there the laird ; and his being in residence was so much the natural thing that strangers were surprised at the apparent indifference with which the people on the estate treated his presence among them. In the country, living a family life on his own place among his own people, King George was happiest ; and for all who loved him there is consolation in the thought that the end came peacefully upon him in the home that he loved best. But on that love of home, on that country life of practical knowledge and detailed interest, hung much more than his personal happiness. Half a thought spared to Versailles, to the *villégiature* of the Trianon, and the pinchbeck rusticities of the Petit Trianon and the Hameau reveals the gulf between two conceptions of kingship. One affirms the unlikeness of Royalty to the rest of humanity ; the other affirms its likeness. Out of the common pleasures, occupations, and interests of life it builds up its towering ideal of service. Starting with the nearest and simplest duties to immediate dependents, it unfolds with increasing opportunity increasing obligation, until a vast Empire is ruled in the same spirit as a country estate.

Yesterday the squire of Sandringham left home for the last time. He will be at home no more until he is laid to rest in what, by convention, is his last home, where he will sleep with his father and his mother, and the beloved sister whose funeral he attended but a few weeks ago. The second stage of his last journey marked a change. When the train arrived in London those who were assembled to meet it were awaiting not the squire of Sandringham but King George of England. But not yet had the full pomp and state of Empire claimed him. The Imperial Crown was laid upon the coffin ; but the mourners—The King, the Princes of the blood Royal, and certain members of the Royal household—went on foot, bare-headed and in plain clothes. Queen Mary (for twenty-five years " Queen Mary " to her people, and for many years to come, it may be hoped, " Queen Mary " still) with the other Royal ladies drove round another way to the common destination. It was not, then, the Crown, not any form of grandeur, of grace, or of splendour, but the shortness, the severity of the procession, which held the eye and impressed the mind. At the far end of the slow and solemn journey more august honours awaited the dead Monarch. For the moment, in the streets of London, with the plain London crowd, in all its immobility and inexpressiveness under sorrow, massed, silent and still, upon the pavements, the object of the general grief and reverence could not be the country gentleman, yet did not seem to be the ruler of the Empire. It was the King of England, passing for the last time through the capital of England. There were Kings of England long before there was a British Empire ; and King George, as we have lately read, was so proud of nothing as of the antiquity of his kingly office, and his birthright as an Englishman. Yesterday afternoon, in the dim and wintry light, London, which but a few months ago had cheered and waved to her King, as smiling and erect he drove through the sunshine and the gaiety of flags and streamers, gathered him once more to her heart in silence and in awe, as, silent himself now and still, he passed through his capital on the second stage of his last journey.

The goal was Westminster Hall, where the Royal coffin was to be received by the Archbishop of Canterbury and other great officers of State, and where the King, Queen Mary, and other members of the Royal Family were to see it laid on the catafalque —Crown and Orb and Sceptre now proclaiming the utmost dignity of the dead King—and to say the first prayers beside its couch of State. To Westminster Hall only last May King George and Queen Mary had come in full pomp and ceremony to receive addresses from the Houses of Parliament. In Westminster Hall yesterday the Lords and Commons met again to do honour to King George. In that Hall, which for centuries has played a high part in the Parliamentary history of England, Parliament assembled to bid farewell to a Sovereign who, under conditions more difficult than any known to his predecessors, walked with steady step the strict constitutional path, and by his wisdom increased the influence of the Throne while enlarging the liberties of the people. In the Commons before the ceremony in Westminster Hall, in the Lords after it, the virtues of the dead King were celebrated by speakers stirred to their finest utterance by sincere conviction and deep feeling. They spoke of his courage, his understanding, his moderation, his personal power. " Strong in his own faith," said Lord Halifax in the Lords, " he was able to inspire others with a courage which matched his own." " His sense of duty to his people," said the Prime Minister, " amounted to genius." " He was the supreme exponent," said Mr. Attlee, the Leader of the Opposition, " of the difficult art of constitutional kingship." Thus, with tributes of admiration and love from those who best knew his difficulties, his qualities, and his achievement,

73

and with words of sympathy for his bereaved Queen and family, of high hope and confidence for his heir, there ended the second stage of the last journey of the country gentleman, the King of England, the ruler of the mightiest and the happiest Empire that the world has known. And, before these lines are read, hundreds of the people for whom King George lived and toiled will have begun to gather together to pay him their last respects.

THE LAST AUDIENCE

KING GEORGE THE FIFTH lies in Westminster Hall, taking what the Prime Minister has reminded us is the only rest of Kings. On either side of him, from early morning till a late hour of night, passes a continuous stream of men and women—myriads upon myriads, without haste and without pause —the " very dear people " who received his message of love at Christmas, who rejoiced with him in the sunlit days of Jubilee, and who come now in silence and sadness to salute him and take leave. The stream began to flow before dawn yesterday morning, from a source beyond Lambeth Bridge ; and it will flow on steadily to-day and for two days more, until it may be that nearly a million of the late King's subjects have made their obeisance. They will be but a small fraction of the innumerable hosts, dwelling in the uttermost bounds of his wide dominions, whose hearts turn to Westminster Hall to-day.

The King lies in death, as he moved in life, in the midst of symbols—historic, majestical, and holy. Around him stand the armed men who guarded his throne, with swords and axes and halberds, with plumed helmets and Elizabethan ruffs, typifying the pride and prowess of his people, who have kept in his reign and under his leadership their unsullied honour and inviolate shores. Over the tall catafalque is draped the Royal Standard, the emblem that links him with his ancestors, who first rode with the golden leopards on their shields in hope to free the Holy Sepulchre. It stands also for the union of all the once hostile peoples of the British Isles, a union of which the King's person is the warranty and the seal. On the standard lie the symbols of his fullest majesty—the sceptre, the orb, and the Imperial Crown—representing so large and various a sway over free and separate nations as has been given to no other King ever anointed to rule over men. The great hall in which he lies is itself a symbol, associated as it has been for so many centuries with the central traditions of the

State, but especially with Parliamentary governance and with the administration of that even-handed justice which is the distinctive English contribution to the political betterment of mankind. The eye, however, turns swiftly away from these mighty abstractions, and rests upon a gentler symbol, the frail wreath of white and pink flowers that lies beside the massy gold of orb and crown. The Queen, who stands nearest to the person of the Sovereign, is also the first of his subjects, and in the token of her love and grief for the man each of them may see his own affection recorded. So thought travels to the other symbols, whose significance lies above and beyond all earthly majesty—to where the candles burn for parable of a flame that death shall not quench, and where at the King's head, soaring above crown and standards, lights and swords, the Cross of his Redeemer stands serene in benediction. From that most significant of all the symbols it is but a little step in thought to the realization that that which lies beneath the silken draperies, and within the oaken casket, is itself now no more than a symbol. For the reality of which it was once the vessel,

> we believe him
> Something far advanced in State
> And that he wears a truer crown
> Than any wreath that man can weave him.

Yet, surrounded by august and consecrated symbolism as King George lies, it is not to the symbols that the thousands do reverence. The farewell is not to the Crown, but to the King. A kindly smile to a humble subject brought into momentary contact with majesty, an inflexion of the broadcast voice at Christmastime, things like these mean more in retrospect to those who pass by than the great acts of State for which the visible emblems stand. Even so, these things are more closely related to the symbols and the abstractions than they seem. The multitudinous feet pass on ; from the doors of Westminster Hall they go their divergent ways, and carry with them on their several paths towards the grave the various memories of King George, his wisdom and kindliness, his industry and fortitude, his courtesy and broad humanity, his lifelong devotion to the service of God and men. In a few decades they will all be gone, and there will be nothing left of King George but a chapter in the history books and a tradition added to the symbols of Royalty. History will merge the man in the institution. Nevertheless the institution is what the man causes it to be. To realize this it is but necessary to reflect for a moment on that Imperial emblem on the catafalque, and consider what at different epochs the Crown has meant in Westminster Hall. King William Rufus, who built the Hall, died execrated by all men in the New Forest; King Richard of Bordeaux, who renewed it, was thrust down from his throne by civil mutiny; when King Charles faced his judges there the Crown had been trampled in the blood and mire of internal strife; while the fourth George, holding his coronation banquet, came there triumphant over his own Queen after the last unseemly episode of a long public brawl. From that depth of moral abasement the Crown has been exalted in the last hundred years to its present commanding dominion over the hearts and minds of men, not by any irresistible and impersonal current of history, but simply by the queenly and kingly virtues of the three generations of human beings who have worn it since 1837. The great Hall itself, in which the King lies in state, is an image of these things. There is nothing in its towering and majestic splendours that was not in the vision of the architects, in the industry and craftsmanship of the nameless masons, the staunchness of the rock whence its stones were hewn. These virtues have been built into the noble fabric, and so preserved through the centuries.

In like manner is it with our potent symbol of the Crown. As an institution it has not some mysterious virtue of its own, over and above the virtues of the individuals who have made its history. Among those individuals must be accounted not only the Sovereigns who have worn it but the subjects who have served it; for kingship is not exercised in a void. There cannot be a great King without a great people; but when a people has proved its greatness under great leadership, as this people most assuredly has done during the past reign, then the fruit of its faith and its valour is linked to the achievement of its ancestors and handed down to its posterity through its continuing institutions. Among these institutions none is of richer content than the Crown, and no man has more enriched the tradition than he whom we mourn. Therefore, when a generation yet unborn come to Westminster Hall and ask, " What mean these stones ? " the answer that must be given to them will dwell with proud remembrance upon the name of King George the Fifth and the people who served him, loved him, and are parting from him now.

CHAPTER IV

THE BURIAL OF THE KING

UNPRECEDENTED crowds watched in reverent silence the final passing of King George V through the streets of London on January 28, on the processional way to Windsor for his burial. A sailor King, he was appropriately borne home by bluejackets, who drew from Westminster Hall to Paddington the gun-carriage on which the coffin lay. Behind the coffin walked King Edward and his brothers, with Royal and other mourners from many lands. Queen Mary and the other ladies of the Royal Family followed in carriages. Representative detachments of the Defence Forces of the Empire made an impressive display in the funeral procession, which gained in colour and variety by the inclusion of officers of the corresponding forces of more than thirty foreign Powers. The streets were lined by police and troops who at some of the more densely crowded points were hard pressed at times to preserve the route from encroachment by the massed ranks of the spectators. The world shared the Empire's sorrow and leave-taking of King George. In every land memorial services were held, and in many impressive ways noble tribute was paid to the late King's memory. The Empire was united in homage and remembrance. The Two Minutes Silence, which began at 1.30 p.m., was observed everywhere.

" Man goeth to his long home, and the mourners go about the streets."

They were about the streets of London, the mourners of King George, in their hundreds, as early as midnight on Monday, January 27, and in their tens of thousands by 2 o'clock on the morning of the funeral.

At that chill time the kerbs were thinly fringed with them along both sides of the more companionable thoroughfares, such as Whitehall, St. James's Street, Piccadilly, and Edgware Road through which the procession would pass, and columns of them, slight as yet but continuous, walked rapidly up and down seeking good positions before settling down to the long wait. Their number was steadily increased by those who had made their pilgrimage through Westminster Hall, which was open long after midnight, and had chosen to go on to see the dead King's last journey through London rather than return home by the omni-buses which were parked in scores awaiting them on the Embankment and the streets off Whitehall.

These earliest arrivals gathered most thickly in the neighbour-hood of Westminster Hall and in Whitehall. They sat along the stone balustrades of some of the Government offices and upon every refuse bin. They leaned upon the whole length of the long pavement guard-rail opposite to the Cenotaph, and sat upon the kerb. Some lay quietly down and slept, wrapped in rugs or newspapers. Whole families were present. In some cases they had brought kitchen chairs with them. Along the Mall every lamp standard was the centre of a little group of patiently resting people. At 2 o'clock in Piccadilly there were still workmen busy putting the finishing touches to stands for spectators, and in Edgware Road many more, whose tasks also included the completion of the removal of every one of the long line of street island refuges.

No doubt a great proportion of this early multitude were eager to see a majestic spectacle ; their presence so many hours before the event showed that. Yet the desire is a very human one, and their demeanour otherwise, in all their haste to be in front for the pageant, showed them also mindful that their being there was firstly a tribute of respect and loyal sympathy. Few people had failed to put themselves into the decent mourning expected of them ; in most cases even those in light-coloured clothes at least wore black armbands or hats or neckties.

After about 3.30 the trains began to arrive at the main line termini from a score of different and distant parts of England and Wales. Heavy rain came with the daylight. About 7 o'clock the stationary hosts and the hurrying columns of the later arrivals endured a fairly thorough wetting, in spite of umbrellas that seemed to be possessed by at least one in every five. In three-quarters of an hour or so the rain stopped, though there were two or three lighter showers later.

The citizens of the Royal Borough of Windsor also were stirring at an early hour. From midnight for some time heavy rain fell, but by 4 o'clock it had stopped, and though the last journey of the dead King through the town would be made at least three hours after the departure from Westminster Hall there were already many signs of activity. Lights gleamed from windows all over the grey old Castle and in many houses where people were getting up, and groups of people were established along the kerbs.

Under grey skies, with slow, sad pageantry, the funeral procession of King George V passed through the streets of the Capital ; and a vast concourse, dark and silent, took sorrowing and proud farewell of a leader under whose inspiration the nation had ridden out a quarter of a century of unexampled storms. Gratitude for a life spent in service, sorrow for the loss of one who had, time and again, proved himself a true friend to his subjects of every class and creed—these were perhaps the dominant emotions felt alike by high and low as the long column, moving to the throb of muffled drums and the sweet elegiac music of the massed bands or the shrill lamentings of the pipes, defiled with infinite sadness and dignity from Westminster to Paddington.

Those who saw the procession as but one stage in a stately progress to a splendid climax saw it truly. The progress was to end in the chapel of St. George's, Windsor, the private chapel of the Order of the Garter, the conception, if not the formula, of which goes back to the beginning of English history and links itself to the order of chivalry that sat at King Arthur's Round Table. There, amid banners and pennants, robes, and uniforms blazing and glowing with colours of historic significance, attended by every circumstance of regal state, his knightly " achievements " sonorously proclaimed by Garter Principal King of Arms, King George was laid to rest as the Sovereign of the Order, the Ruler of a great Empire, the inheritor of centuries of majestic tradition in which kings may die but the King ever lives.

Along the whole distance of the processional route in London the dark shining streets were lined by the soldiers of many regiments—a curving, vari-coloured hedge. Along part of the way —Whitehall, St. James's Street, and Piccadilly—stood tall purple-swathed mourning masts with flowing purple bannerettes capped by black crêpe. Panels of black or purple appeared on the front

The procession crossing the Horse Guards Parade.

of balconies, and, while police barricades were white, shop window barricades were uniformly black or purple. Otherwise no attempt had been made to give the procession a formal setting. Shops were closed ; windows were crowded ; railings and trees were perched upon by late-comers, some of the trees in Hyde Park looking like rookeries ; and almost every roof thrust up an irregular line of silhouettes against the slowly paling sky.

To go back over the day is to recall first of all, perhaps, the mingling of bells, the solemn strokes of Big Ben, which began a quarter of an hour before the coffin was borne out of West-minster Hall on the shoulders of Guardsmen, and the peals that spoke from the tower of Westminster Abbey of life and immortality. And then every one, from his own place, must carry an ineffaceable impression of long successive patterns of colour, broadening down from the glitter of the dismounted cavalry through the heavy gold of bandsmen and varying shades of blue to khaki, passing smoothly and in stately manner between the dark banks of people, as though gently floating on a wide, shining river. And at length the sailor-drawn gun-carriage, which had borne Queen Victoria and King Edward VII, now lifting high the coffin of King George. Draped in the Royal Standard, it supported the Imperial Crown, the Orb and Sceptre, and the late King's insignia of the Order of the Garter. Beside these emblems of earthly greatness lay a single wreath. Part of this impression is the King, in naval uniform, with his Royal brothers following the bier at the head of a brilliant group of Kings, Princes and accredited envoys of exalted rank and high personal distinction. For some, especially those on the rearward fringes of the crowd, the great State carriages in which the Queen and the Royal ladies were sitting may also take firm lodgment in the memory. With the coachmen and clinging footmen, each a billow of scarlet, they caught the fugitive gleams of sunshine that fell upon the procession in Hyde Park.

The procession left Westminster Hall at 9.45, and there the special quality of the scene was its continuing silence, unbroken by music to the last or by any sound but of Big Ben and the tolling of bells.

Horse Guards moving out to their position near to the Victoria Tower were the first indication of that rearward part of the procession which had formed, or was forming, to the west.

G

Beyond their single brilliance of colour darker sections of waiting
men were now to be distinguished. Officers began to arrive in
Palace Yard ; the guard of honour, drawn from the 1st Battalion,
Grenadier Guards, the Royal Marines, and the Royal Air Force,
moved into position facing Westminster Hall ; and outside the
gates the massed pipers assembled. Beyond them formed a long
line of members of foreign delegations and their attached suites.
The Gentlemen at Arms were posted at the gates themselves.

At about a quarter past nine the Royal mourners from foreign
countries had begun to arrive, and soon afterwards the Royal
Dukes and the King himself, accompanied by King Leopold.
The gun-carriage was brought out and withdrawn again. Queen
Mary, with Queen Maud of Norway, the Princess Royal and the
Duchess of York, arrived in a glass coach, which drove up to
the steps of Westminster Hall, and was followed by a second
coach and six State landaus into Palace Yard. There was now a
brief pause, the crowd still and expectant. The gun-carriage was
brought out a second time, the crew standing, now bare-headed,
eight abreast, the white drag-ropes in their hands. Rain had
ceased and the cloud-rift momentarily lightened, covering the
scene, not in sunlight, for the sun did not break through, but in a
bleak, luminous glare.

Beneath the awning outside the entrance to Westminster Hall
the bearers were seen with their burden. The coffin was carried
slowly forward. As it slid into place on the gun-carriage the
sound of its movement, intervening between the tolling of bells,
was for an instant faintly audible across the width of Palace Yard,
so deep was the accompanying silence. Except to a watcher from
above or from within the Yard itself, this part of the ceremony
was hidden by the slope of the ground and by the interposition of
the guard of honour, but soon the advanced part of the procession
and the great officers of the Household began to move forward,
and the gun's crew followed. As the coffin, and the King behind
it, passed out of Palace Yard, the Royal Standard, which had
been flying at half-mast above the Houses of Parliament, was
struck and the Union Jack broken in its place.

As the procession moved into Parliament Square there was
little colour ; except of the tread of feet, muffled by the road-
sand, and of the continuing bells, there was no sound. The crowd
ceased to sway, a rustle passed through them as of corn that the
breeze touches, and they became still. The gun's crew and the

bearer-parties beside them came on, the seamen marching with faultless precision but, even at the slow, with that looseness of rhythm which distinguishes their march from soldiers'.

Behind the gun-carriage a warrant officer of the Household cavalry bore the Royal Standard, followed by the King, in naval great-coat, walking alone and erect, but heavily, the strain of the past week and of the previous night's vigil being visible in him. He was followed by the Dukes of York, Gloucester, and Kent, by the President of the French Republic, by the Royal mourners from abroad, by the Marquess of Carisbrooke, Prince Arthur of Connaught, and other members of the House of Windsor, all on foot.

Queen Mary's coach, which by its sudden colour lit the scene, preceded a group of High Commissioners and representatives of foreign States. Behind them, stretching into the distance, was a long line of foreign delegations, civil, military, and naval, and beyond these the head of the third division of the escort. For twenty-five minutes they moved past—the escort, the sombre police contingent, the fire brigade contingent, and finally, the last of the Horse Guards—the church bells still their only music.

In Whitehall and Parliament Street the people were massed ten deep upon the pavements and every window in the Government offices was filled. The Senior Service, which lined the first part of the route, made a border of dark blue and white up the wide road and round the curve into the Horse Guards. Behind them in black and white stood the men of the St. John Ambulance.

More than an hour before the procession was due to leave sections were being marshalled in the roadway. Far up beyond the Cenotaph were the Air Council and the high officers of the Royal Air Force ; next the Army Council, the Generals and Field-Marshals ; and by the Cenotaph itself the Board of Admiralty and a group of Admirals, among whom was Lord Beatty. Between them and the massed bands, led by that of the Royal Air Force, stood the Aides-de-Camp to his late Majesty. Precisely at the appointed time they began to move off at the slow march. As they reached the spot where on Armistice Day King George had so often stood to honour the dead the officers saluted to the music now of pipes, now of military bands, and the procession went slowly on. The Royal coffin lifted high and catching the eye from afar, with the rich colours of the Standard and the flashing jewels of the Imperial Crown, was like a tall ship floating upon a moving tide of men.

Outside St. James's Palace a vast multitude had gathered, and here, though barricades had been early fixed in position, special steps had to be taken successfully to marshal the crowd. Even so, just before the procession went by so great was the press that the lines bulged perilously outwards. In Piccadilly the crowds were incredibly large ; Hyde Park held its thousands, but it was at Marble Arch that the greatest concourse gathered, and there the route was kept only with difficulty. Many fainted ; children were passed out over the heads of the crowd ; the ambulance men were in constant demand. In the utmost discomfort and often definitely in fear the multitude waited, pushed hither and thither, swaying, straining. A puff of grey smoke from the distance and almost immediately the first thud of gunfire told them at length that their vigil was drawing to an end.

Large crowds gathered from an early hour outside Paddington Station. They were thick from the junction of London Street, and the Oxford and Cambridge Terrace. Praed Street was barricaded at each end of London Street. The end of the inclined way leading down into Paddington Station had its pavement barricaded. By 9 o'clock every point of vantage had been taken.

After the head of the procession, an officer of the Headquarter Staff followed closely by two very tall Life Guards, had come round the corner into the little square leading to the incline down into the station, there was a long gap. Then came the First and Second Division of Escort, and soon detachment was following detachment until it seemed that there would be no end. All this time not a sound was heard but the tread of feet on the sanded slope. The Earl Marshal appeared and, a few moments later, the Naval Crew. Then the gun-carriage came into view and, slowly and in state, sank down towards the darkness of the station. The King and his brothers, other Kings and potentates, and the Royal coaches followed and vanished into the gloom.

At Paddington, the funeral train, coupled to the engine Windsor Castle, which King George himself had once driven when he visited the Great Western Railway works at Swindon, stood waiting. To the funeral music of military bands the gun-carriage was brought alongside. Queen Mary's glass coach stopped near the funeral compartment of the train. The band ceased, and with that the clatter of hoofs and trundling wheels became audible,

84

even noisy.   The King went to the door of the leading carriage, and his mother and the other Royal occupants descended, and Princess Elizabeth joined her parents.

The bearer party lifted the coffin to their shoulders, and bore it slowly to the train, between two lines of mourning Royalty. Now a band in the distance was playing " O Rest in the Lord." The King, Queen Mary, and the others went to their compartments.   The starting signal, far down the platform, turned from orange to green.

The train left Paddington at 12.31, half an hour late.   Four minutes afterwards there was a last glimpse of it as it rounded the curve beyond the station, its woodwork shining in a chequered sunlight.

Throughout the morning, Windsor Station was a scene of quiet and orderly activity.   It was closed to the public at an early hour, and thereafter the final arrangements for King George's last journey were carried out.   The pillars on the platform of arrival were draped in purple.   In the Royal waiting room the picture of the late King had been similarly decorated, and white lilies stood in vases on the table and on the mantelpiece over a cheerful fire.   But otherwise no attempt had been made to transform the appearance of the interior of the station.

Five special trains came into Windsor before the Royal train carrying the coffin and the Royal mourners.   The first four trains brought visitors, who proceeded at once to St. George's Chapel. Within a few minutes there arrived most of the leaders of political thought of the present generation.   The Prime Minister, Lord Hailsham, Mr. Chamberlain, Mr. Lloyd George, Mr. Attlee, Sir Archibald Sinclair, Mr. Eden, Mr. Churchill, Mr. Runciman, Mr. Lansbury, the Speaker, and Mr. Ramsay MacDonald were among those who went by.   They spoke of overwhelming crowds in London, of difficulties encountered in reaching Paddington ; but they were not aware that the funeral service was likely to be delayed in consequence.   The fourth train brought many of the Ambassadors to the Court of St. James's, among them the representatives of France, Italy, and Soviet Russia.   They were accompanied by Sir Austen Chamberlain and Sir Robert Horne, the chairman of the Great Western Railway, and then it became known to those in the station that the Royal train would not be able to leave Paddington until half an hour after the arranged time, and a long period of waiting began.

In the meantime the 150 men from the Excellent, who were to draw the gun-carriage bearing King George's body, and the guards of honour from the Royal Navy, the Brigade of Guards, and the Royal Air Force had taken up their positions in the station courtyard. A few minutes before 1 o'clock the last of the special trains arrived. It brought many of the foreign representatives who had taken part in the procession through London, and as they assembled on the platform to await the Royal train the picture was one of brilliant colours heightened by the medieval pageantry provided by the Heralds and the Kings of Arms, among whom the figure of Sir Nevile Wilkinson, Ulster King of Arms, who also attended the funeral of King Edward twenty-five years ago in his official capacity, stood out conspicuously.

The funeral train should have reached Windsor at 12.35, but, in fact, it was not until nine minutes past 1 o'clock that it glided into the station, to the accompaniment of the minute guns which told the waiting and anxious crowds of the return of King George to the Royal City. The coach containing the coffin was drawn up within a few yards of the Royal waiting room. Under the direction of the Earl Marshal, the bearer party entered the coach and the coffin was borne reverently across the platform to the gun-carriage. In the stillness the command " Off Caps " rang out, and the men from the Excellent stood with bared heads and hands gripping the drag-ropes as the bearers passed. On the coffin lay the Royal Standard and surmounting it the Crown, the Regalia, the Insignia of the Order of the Garter, and the Queen's wreath. Then for a moment of unforgettable beauty the stillness was broken by the wailing of the bosun's pipe. The Navy was paying its own tribute to the Monarch whom it regarded as its special possession. The bosun's whistle was piping the call " Admiral alongside." A few seconds later, when the coffin had been placed on the gun-carriage, came the second shrill call, " Admiral aboard."

As the sound of the pipe died in the air the final orders were given. The Earl Marshal took his place in the procession, which moved slowly forward to the sound of the Funeral March. As in London, the King walked immediately behind his father's body, with his brothers a pace in the rear. Behind them came the foreign Monarchs and Princes, and then a solitary carriage drawn by a pair of Windsor greys and carrying Queen Mary, Queen Maud of Norway, the Princess Royal, the Duchess of

York, and Princess Elizabeth. The company which had assembled on the platform after the arrival of the last special train joined the procession, and finally came seven cars, in which rode the other Royal ladies, and the sons of the Princess Royal. And so the last progress began, and as the mourners passed out of the station into the crowded High Street the last impression they gathered was of the lowered colours of the eighty branches of the British Legion in the County of Berkshire, all borne by men in civilian clothes who had shared with their dead Monarch the anxieties, the sufferings, and the glories of the Great War.

From the station the funeral passed in regal splendour along Windsor's narrow and crooked High Street between great crowds who had long awaited its coming. The procession was shorter than that which passed through the streets of London ; the splendour was more concentrated and made a picture of solemn grandeur. At 1.30, when the Two Minutes Silence spread over the country and the Empire, the funeral procession was still passing through the gateway into the Home Park to the melancholy music of pipes, and so it wended its way out of sight towards St. George's Chapel.

On arrival at St. George's Chapel the gun-carriage was halted immediately opposite the door. The bearers stepped forward. To the boatswain's piping the coffin was lifted off, and then borne up the steps, while the King and his brothers stood at the salute. The bare gun-carriage moved on. Queen Mary alighted from her carriage and was escorted up the steps by the King. The Dean received the coffin, and the bearers entered the Chapel.

No worthier setting than the Chapel itself could be found for a great King who made his greatness by his simplicity. As the congregation filed slowly in through the small door in the south wall they saw perhaps the most English of all sanctuaries. The great western window threw a flood of cold clean light on the fluted columns of the nave, so delicate that their height seemed a miracle, so exquisitely proportioned that they seemed to have grown, not to have been made. The aisle was covered with a rich blue carpet, on either side of which were set rows of chairs reaching right back to the walls, and standing on a pale-grey floor-cloth, which added to the impression of spaciousness.

On top of the shallow steps leading to the Chancel, which is that part of the Chapel allocated to the Knights of the Garter, stands the oaken screen, with the organ discreetly hidden above and to the sides. Within the Chancel are the stalls of the Knights, each with a banner hung above, and with the coats of arms of successive occupants inlaid upon brass and let into the back panelling. The carpet on the floor hid the tombs of several Kings, including that of Charles I, and a picture arose in the mind, in contrast to the great concourse of to-day, of his hurried sepulture in a flurry of snow by a few bitter mourners nearly 300 years ago.

On the left of the altar, looking East, behind a superbly wrought iron grille, was the tomb of Edward IV, the first King to be buried in the chapel ; and above it was the box in carved oak with coats of arms blazoned on the panels which Henry VIII caused to be made for Catherine of Aragon. On the right were the tomb and recumbent effigies of Edward VII and his Queen. The altar itself was draped with a cloth of finest gold tapestry, and on it were a few bunches of lilies, no lovelier than the columns which soared upwards to blossom into the tracery of the roof.

Such was the setting in which a noble company assembled to pay a last tribute to King George V. Dark cloaks hid the brilliance of the uniforms, and the mourning veils of the ladies gave the congregation a sombre tint. The most noticeable section of it in the body of the Chapel was the phalanx of His Majesty's Judges in their wigs and robes.

In the stalls of the Choir the Knights of the Garter took their places with their ladies, the first to arrive being Lord Derby, followed by Lord Halifax and Sir Austen Chamberlain. Members of the Cabinet, including Mr. Baldwin and Mr. Ramsay MacDonald, took most of the vacant places. And there was something incongruous in even the brilliant uniform of a Privy Councillor beneath the signs of an older chivalry—the helmets and visors fixed on top of the canopy of the stalls and the banners blazing with colours. The rest of the stalls had been given to those who had rendered great service during King George's reign, among them Mr. Lloyd George. Only the stall of the Sovereign of the Order was empty and unadorned. That of the Queen was also empty, but veiled and covered.

All through the hours of waiting there was an impressive silence and a sensation in all hearts that the congregation had come to say farewell to a friend, not to be mere spectators of a gorgeous ceremony.

At last, through an archway on the north side of the choir came the ecclesiastical procession, which advanced with measured tread to the main entrance. It was headed by the Archbishop of Canterbury, walking side by side with the Dean of Windsor —for no Bishop or Archbishop has jurisdiction over the Chapel. Behind came the Archbishop of York and the Canons of the Chapel, the former in black and gold, the latter in murrey cassocks with the Cross of St. George on a white ground on their left shoulder. The copes worn by the Archbishops were those first used for the funeral of Charles II. Both Archbishops displayed their primatial crosses as a matter of courtesy and not as a right ; and southerners in the congregation had the unusual sight of the splendid cross of York being carried in procession south of the Trent.

The wait at the western door was a long one, for the arrival at Windsor had been about forty minutes late, and for this reason the Two Minutes Silence could not be observed in the Chapel. During the interval, other ladies in deepest mourning came, headed by Queen Victoria Eugénie of Spain, and took their places in the Choir ; and there, after the procession had entered, they were joined by the Royal Duchesses, Princess Elizabeth holding her mother's hand, and the two sons of the Princess Royal in kilts of the Royal tartan. Just beyond the screen on either side of the entrance to the Chancel were stationed the Military Knights of Windsor in their cocked hats with abrupt little red and white plumes. In marched the Officers of Arms, with their richly embroidered tabards—all the English Pursuivants and Heralds and the five Kings of Arms, including Ulster and the Lord Lyon, who had come to accompany their English brethren. They formed up just in front of the Military Knights.

Presently there floated into the Chapel the faint thunder of the funeral march played by the massed band of the Guards. It died away, and through the door came the shrill blast of the bosun's pipe as the coffin was " piped over the side " at the foot of the steps. As it was borne up to the entrance the skirl of Highland pipes took up the mourning music, and to their high, exultant wailing the coffin passed through the door. The whole congregation rose to their feet and looked with reverence and pity at two beyond all others of the mighty procession that paced slowly up to the chancel steps. These two were first King Edward VIII, with his set face from which all the boyish and nervous glow of the Prince of Wales had vanished in a few brief days, and, secondly, Queen Mary, erect, stately, and infinitely sad. *Et vera incessu patuit regina.*

As the procession advanced the choir at its head broke into a chanting of the magnificent and uplifting promises, " I am the resurrection and the life " and " I know that my Redeemer liveth "—words almost too thrilling to be sung. Slowly they mounted the steps, slowly swung to the right as the clergy swung to the left, and slowly the bearers placed the coffin on the purple covered bier at the foot of the steps leading to the altar. There followed a pause, while the bearers lifted the Crown, Orb and Sceptre, carried them to a small dais prepared on the left of the altar steps, and replaced them with a mass of flowers, placed ready to hand by the Comptroller of the Household.

King Edward and his mother stood motionless behind the coffin. Behind them, right to the doors, stood the long line of Kings, Presidents, Princes, and leaders of nations. Suddenly the choir, whose singing throughout was beyond praise, broke into the psalm of comfort, " The Lord is my Shepherd." As the last note died away the Bishop of Winchester, as Prelate of the Order of the Garter, moved to the foot of the coffin, and in a clear but clearly moved voice read the lesson from Revelation, with its solemn assurance " there shall be no more death." Again the choir took up the service with the dead King's favourite hymn, " Abide with me," the great singer of which, Dame Clara Butt, also passed away only a few days ago.

Then the deep tones of the Archbishop of Canterbury uttered the terrible words, a reminder of the frailty of man, which precede committal of the body to the earth. The coffin sank slowly down into the vault through the floor to its resting place. King Edward stepped forward and cast a handful of earth upon it. Then, while all hearts were wrung for him at that bitter moment, the Archbishop of Canterbury pronounced the formula of committal. " Earth to earth, ashes to ashes, dust to dust " ; but " in the sure and certain hope of the resurrection to eternal life."

His place was taken by the Archbishop of York, who read the prayers for the departed. Then stood forth the Garter Principal King of Arms, who, with a touch of most endearing nervousness, pronounced the styles of both the dead and of the living King.

As the sonorous titles rolled through the Chapel, all felt that sorrow at a noble ending yielded a little to confidence in a noble beginning and to comfort in the continuity of the British monarchy, and many lips moved in soundless echo of the final cry, " God Save the King." A last prayer for divine aid in life and death was chanted by the choir, and the Archbishop of Canterbury, Primate of All England, pronounced the benediction. So ended a service deeply impressive in its simplicity, in the appeal of its music, in the high courage of the chief mourners, and in the reverent sincerity alike of the officiants and of the congregation.

King Edward passed out with his mother. After they had gone the kings and representatives of foreign Powers one by one advanced, bowed towards the rectangle of purple carpet that now covered the tomb, and went out through the north door of the chancel. The rest of the congregation, without formality, slowly filed out, each by the nearest door. In a few moments the chapel was empty. From the cloisters there stole in the sweet incense of the masses of flowers, banked high on the ancient walls. The King had been laid to rest.

*   *   *   *   *

Most remarkable scenes in Windsor followed the passing of the funeral procession. As soon as the rearguard of Yeomen in their Tudor costume had disappeared into the Park the troops which had lined the route were marched away and the crowds surged across the High Street. Their numbers were swollen by the other crowds now released from the side streets, and Thames Street, the High Street, and Park Street were quickly filled from wall to wall with a solid mass of persons. Nothing like that had ever been seen in Windsor and the number of people must have been in the neighbourhood of 100,000. Just when this multitude was beginning to jostle noisily a dramatic thing happened. From wireless loud-speakers which had been installed at the Town Hall there came a broadcast commentary on the approach of the funeral procession to St. George's Chapel, with the music of a Funeral March, and the crowd at once stopped quietly to listen.

There followed the words of the Burial Office and the singing of the choir in St. George's Chapel. Every word and every note was distinctly heard right along the High Street and scores of thousands of people turned instinctively towards the Town Hall and stood in complete silence. The men were bareheaded, and in all this vast crowd of people, tightly wedged forty abreas along the whole length of the High Street, there was not a sound to be heard as the broadcast of the service proceeded.

Just as the crowd first paused to listen to the broadcast an officer with a double file of soldiers attempted to march down the middle of the High Street towards the station. The massed crowd made a passage impossible and he halted his men where they stood. They were completely hemmed in by the crowd for three-quarters of an hour, and it was not until there had been heard the closing words of the Archbishop's Benediction that they were able to resume their march.

But it was not only in Windsor that the broadcast of the funeral service was heard; countless numbers of persons the world over were enabled by radio if not to swell the number of those who by their physical presence took part in a final act of respect and devotion to King George, at any rate to join themselves at will in unity of feeling with mourners everywhere. For where all minds are focused on one place, to one thought, at the same time, there a fellowship is formed. *Magni corporis membra fuimus.*

The broadcasts of the procession in London, admirably done, were made by means of six microphones outside Westminster Hall and three microphones at St. James's Palace. There were sixteen microphones (including those in St. George's Chapel) at Windsor. There were also two microphones in Hyde Park to pick up the sound of the minute guns.

The following countries relayed the funeral service from Windsor, and descriptions from either Westminster Hall or Windsor :

France, Belgium, Holland, Norway, Sweden, Denmark, Austria, Hungary, Czechoslovakia, Poland, Italy, Germany, Japan, Manchukuo, Egypt, North and South America, Dutch East Indies, Switzerland, Algeria, Latvia, Lithuania, Finland, Rumania, Morocco, and Yugoslavia.

Reports of good reception of the broadcasts from Westminster Hall and St. James's Palace were received from Oslo, Copenhagen, Stockholm, Berlin, Vienna, Prague, Budapest, Paris, Brussels, Amsterdam, and Tokyo. Excellent reception of the broadcast from Windsor was reported from Berlin, Budapest, Vienna, Brussels, Paris, Milan, Copenhagen, Oslo, Prague, Kaunas, and Stockholm. Reception was reported as satisfactory from Canada, Australia, India, and South Africa. Reception in the United States of America was also excellent.

For many days after the funeral of King George thousands made pilgrimage to see the masses of flowers—tributes from the highest and the lowest, far and near—that had been sent to Windsor.

The procession passing along Piccadilly.

QUEEN MARY'S MESSAGE

QUEEN MARY'S MESSAGE

Queen Mary addressed the following message to
the Nation on the day after the funeral:

I MUST send to you, the people of this Nation and Empire, a
message of my deepest gratitude for all the sympathy with which
at this time of sorrow you have surrounded me. It is indeed a
gratitude so deep that I cannot find words to express it. But the
simplest words are the best. I can only say with all my heart I
thank you.

In my own great sorrow I have been upheld not only by the
strength of your sympathy but also by the knowledge that you
have shared my grief. For I have been deeply moved by the signs
so full and touching that the passing of my dear husband has
brought a real sense of personal sorrow to all his subjects. In the
midst of my grief I rejoice to think that after his Reign of twenty-
five years he lived to know that he had received the reward in
overflowing measure of the loyalty and love of his people.

Although he will be no longer at my side—and no words can
tell how I shall miss him—I trust that with God's help I may still
be able to continue some part at least of the service which for
forty-two years of happy married life we tried together to give to
this great land and Empire. During the coming years, with all the
changes which they must bring, you will, I know, let me have a
place in your thoughts and prayers.

I commend to you my dear son as he enters upon his Reign, in
confident hope that you will give to him the same devotion and
loyalty which you gave so abundantly to his father.

God bless you, dear people, for all the wonderful love and
sympathy with which you have sustained me.

MARY.

LEADING ARTICLES FROM "THE TIMES"

H

"THIS OUR BROTHER"

IN the service broadcast on Sunday there was recited the collect from the Order for the Burial of the Dead, which will be read over the King's grave at Windsor, which is read indeed over great and lowly alike when their bodies are committed to the earth. Its central petition is " that, when we shall depart this life, we may rest in Him, as our hope is this our brother doth." While King George lived it was natural to think of him as the father of his people. But in the presence of the universal Fatherhood, to whose loving kindness we now commit him, he is no more—and no less—than the brother of all Christian men. It is easy and comforting so to think of " this simple and truly humble man," as the Archbishop of Canterbury has called him. He has laid aside all his dignities, in the spirit of one who never mistook them for anything more than a ceremonial garment or allowed them to muffle the beating of a warm and sensitive heart. His people see him, as undoubtedly he saw himself, as one of their own kind, an ordinary man called upon to play an extraordinary part. In taking up the heavy burden of his office he was not helped by any outstanding gifts of intellectual eminence. He had not even received an education specially devised to equip him for the responsibilities of a King. Cleverer men, in easier times, had worn the Crown before him, and had shown themselves overburdened by it. King George, armed only with the powers of the average man, had to stand at the head of his people in crisis after crisis, confronting the assaults of adverse circumstance. That he remained undefeated by them all, and came out at last into a little of the calm of victory before the end, means more to his people than would a like triumph achieved by any superhuman genius. They have seen how great is the power latent in the common man, and have been encouraged to believe that, whatsoever call may come to any one of them, if he will but answer it with the faith and courage and humility of King George, he will not fail for lack of natural gifts.

That, after all, has been the lesson of the Empire's experience in this great reign. In war and in peace the British peoples have endured trials and won victories that have been the wonder of the world. They have been victories, not of brilliant generals and statesmen, but of common humanity, and the strength that has won them has been the strength of brotherhood, of which the inspiration has been the King. When the greatest of poets had to present his most heroic figure of a King of England in the crisis of his destiny, he made him hail his followers as his brethren. " We few, we happy few, we band of brothers " is the cry of King Harry on the eve of Agincourt. They who acknowledged King George as their leader on sterner fields than Agincourt were not few ; but it was their happiness to feel that they were a band of brothers, of whom the King was one. With each of them, by natural affection, he seemed to share his royalty, just as by law he shared his dominion ; and each, knowing that of any one of them the like high service might, by other dispensations of Providence, have been required, is helped by the King's memory to think better of himself.

It is still only by a conscious effort that we can speak of the King as a memory and not as a presence. Scarcely a week has elapsed since his life ended ; eleven days ago he was quietly at home at Sandringham, and no whisper of alarm had begun to disturb his people. Then came the first slight hint of catastrophe, swiftly deepening and advancing like the cosmic shadow in an eclipse. The first message spoke of " a cold " ; then of " disquiet " ; then of " anxiety." On the Sunday the shadow seemed to halt ; but it was only for a moment. Next day the King's strength was diminishing, and his life in the evening " moved peacefully towards its close." He " ceased upon the midnight with no pain." Quietly, with a grief too near and simple for much formal demonstration, his people resigned themselves to the loss of their friend and leader. They put on mourning garments. Wistfully, having known him well, they hung upon the words of those who had known him intimately, asking, not for solemn declamation, such as has been recited over the graves of the aloof monarchs of history, but for simple facts and memories about the man they loved. The chiefs of Church and State responded to the nation's mood, and showed that it had been the King's own mood at the last. Having nothing that the pomps of artificial rhetoric need conceal, they told the simple truth about the dead, whether they spoke to the firesides of the people, or from pulpit and rostrum in the formal assemblies of the realm. All that they said moved their hearers to deeper love, pride, and grief.

The King's son was proclaimed as his successor, with glow of heraldic pageantry, like the light of dawn seen upon distant mountain tops from a valley still wrapped in the shadows. Then the King's body came back to his capital, and was carried through the hushed streets, his sons and servants walking bareheaded behind the coffin as in any English village the children of a family follow their father to the grave. During that journey, and during the days and nights that followed, when countless thousands of his subjects filed before him in the great Hall of his Palace of Westminster, the King seemed to lie surrounded by a luminous cloud of his people's love,

> Spread round him as round earth soft heaven is spread,
> And peace more strong than death round all the dead.

Those who could take personal leave in the dead King's presence were but the representatives of a far vaster company ; in every corner of the world where men profess the British allegiance the people gathered to do honour to the memory of the departed ; from every land under heaven came messages of sympathy for the bereaved Queen and her children ; and kings, princes, and rulers of the nations assembled in London to pay the last honours that earthly powers can give.

So the King goes on his last journey, out of the crowds and the clangour of his capital, to rest with his ancestors in the venerable peace of Windsor, beside the quiet Thames. For a few more hours he will be surrounded by the utmost of pomp and majesty that immemorial tradition and living reverence can devise to the honour of the beloved dead. Then must he too, " as chimney-sweepers, come to dust." He will lie in the place which, of all others upon earth, is most appropriate to the ideals he has represented in life. This glorious chapel of the Knights of the Garter was built for a monument to the idea of brotherhood in one of its noblest forms—a brotherhood of equal chivalry, under the leadership of a king. Leadership, to-day as in all ages, is a universal need ; the craving for it has led many nations to seek it by strange paths, and the spirit of brotherhood has by some been sacrificed in order to attain it. In these twenty-five crowded troublous, glorious years the peoples of the British Empire have never faltered or lost faith in themselves, because they have always been certain of their leadership. King George learnt and taught the art of the leader whose followers are his brethren, which is both the secret of liberty and the secret of order, and so the answer to the problem of government. " Frater, ave atque vale "—

> good-night, sweet prince,
> And flights of angels sing thee to thy rest.

THE KING'S FUNERAL

THE last valediction is over, and the mortal remains of King George V have been laid to rest in his Castle of Windsor. Yesterday saw the climax of the mourning for the loved and lamented man. First the husband and father, then the lord of an estate, then the King of England, and last the mighty Monarch of a vast world-Power has been mourned, by his family, by his tenants and servants, his kingdom, his Empire, and the world. The simplest of men has been buried with the utmost pomp and splendour in the chapel of the ancient and most noble Order of Chivalry of which he was the hereditary Sovereign. The most modest of men—in his own opinion " a very ordinary sort of fellow "—has been followed to the grave by kings and princes and rulers of the earth, marching afoot through the rain and the sunshine. In this there was nothing incongruous, nothing wasted, nothing merely formal. For one thing, both in the procession and in the funeral service the substance of the pomp and splendour was nothing but the ancient simplicity of the last rites for men of all degrees. For the private soldier, the arms reversed and the slow march ; for the farm labourer or the artisan, the very same words in the church and at the graveside. Further only a creeping materialism or a grinding parsimony can blind itself to the uses of that " useless " custom of ceremonial splendour in joy and in sorrow. Twenty-five years ago in St. George's Chapel King George heard what living ears all the world over might have heard yesterday, the recital by Garter King of Arms of the roll of the King's styles and titles ; and he must have felt then about his father as others felt yesterday about him, that to the passing of a Monarch of so long and illustrious a line, King of such a kingdom, ruler over such an Empire, there was due all that ceremony could devise to express in symbol the antiquity and the height of his earthly grandeur.

Ceremony and splendour do more than that. The plain man, bereaved of a friend, or a relative, puts on a black tie or an arm-band ; his wife does her best, according to her means, to wear "decent" mourning ; and only the express wish of the mourned dissuades them from so doing. Within their own hearts they could mourn just as truly and as deeply in their ordinary clothes. But, if all the world did so, each would mourn alone. The demonstration of sorrow is more than a convention. It is a universal link between all the mourners. It gives to every man, woman, and child the sense of community ; each shares in the grief of all the rest ; those who wear no mourning seem to proclaim themselves outside the pale of the society that is bound together in the common feeling. And the pomp of the funeral procession, the Princes going afoot, the sailors, the soldiers, the military music, the Imperial Crown and Sceptre on the coffin—all this tradition of ritual, jealously guarded from occasion to occasion, and performed with the strictness which gave to that sinuous stream of beauty the oneness of a single being, is in spirit but the black tie, the decent mourning, not of the individual person, not of the Kingdom, not of the Empire, but of the civilized world mourning the loss of a great King and a good man. The death of King George V means a cause of mourning, not to his subjects only, but also to law, order, and constitutional government all the world over. But in the mourning for this our late beloved ruler there has been an element perhaps never so potently present before, an element which has forced itself upon the notice of all who have watched the events of the past eight days. It was no curiosity, no love of spectacle which packed the streets last Thursday with watchers of the little mournful procession from King's Cross to St. Stephen's Hall, so different from the gorgeous train that escorted the body of King Edward VII from Buckingham Palace to the lying-in-state. It was not curiosity nor love of spectacle which brought together yesterday greater crowds than have ever been known in London before, crowds whose sheer weight—English and orderly though they were by nature—broke down the restraining forces of the police at more than one spot on the route. Pomp and ceremony befitted the last journey of the mightiest Monarch in the world, because in pomp

The Queen in the procession to Paddington.

The gun-carriage passing through Hyde Park.

and ceremony the people saw the fulfilment of their own desire to pay the last honours to a father and a friend whom they revered and loved.

King George died just before midnight on Monday, January 20. Since then the trivial round, the common task, have for the public in general gone on much as usual; yet these eight days have in some degree seemed like a respite from the insistence of the petty detail, the ruthless routine of life. They have offered a time of reflection, a breathing-space in which, while we carried on our daily round, we could still look back over the years in which King George V was our supreme head and guardian. And such has been his effect upon the temper of his times that we may look back in something of the glow of that serenity in which he passed from mortal life. To turn up again what was said of him on his accession twenty-five years ago is to see hopes realized and faith confirmed in a manner not common in mortal affairs. What was known for certain then of the new King was as nothing compared with what is known now; and, though public affairs at home and abroad gave cause for uneasiness, none could tell then that at home and abroad his reign was to be beset with struggles more deathly and dangers more awful than any of his predecessors had known. He must mount the Throne at a moment when his own Parliament was in such disorder that reputable persons and journals were begging the Government to spare a young and inexperienced Sovereign the " indecency " of a renewal of the turmoil. In his second year came the " incident " of Agadir; in the third the danger was from Ireland. There is no need to continue the tale. Faith—in his family, perhaps, rather than in himself—encouraged hope; but none could then foresee how one crisis after another (" Will there never be an end of them ? " he cried to the Archbishop of Canterbury in a moment of self-revelation) should break upon him and his people, and how one crisis after another should pass to leave him firmer and still firmer in their admiration, their gratitude, and their love. Twenty-five years ago brave things were said of his Kingdom and his Empire; and none knew then how much braver things there would be to say to-day. Twenty-five years ago it was foretold that he would make a good King; and none could foresee how this simplest and least remote of men would so round out the idea of kingship as to leave it, in all eyes but those of sheer anarchy, a nobler ideal than he found it. He made a good King indeed;

105

but that was not all. Kingship itself is the higher for his example and his achievement.

The last valediction is over, but of this " interred Friend " his faithful people will consent to take no " lasting Adieu." King George rests from his labours ; but his works do follow him. For how long and with how much power they will continue to follow him in the lives of his former subjects and in the history of the great company of nations over which he ruled depends chiefly upon our living selves. The time of reflection is over. To-day the life of plain duties and ordinary cares starts anew. The least among us will do his work the better for cherishing the memory and the example of the late King. But the least of us can do more than that. Above the level of our common grief and effort stand two lonely figures, distinguished by the greatness of their loss no less than by their eminence in earthly dignity. The time will come (as none who knows her may doubt) when Queen Mary will take up again her burden of activity in the service of her people ; but she must take it up again without the chief support of her labours and the chief reward of her success. And King Edward VIII, face to face at last with the drudgery and the responsibility which years of anticipation and preparation can have robbed of little of their threatening aspect—and feeling, perhaps, almost as diffident about matching his father's achievement as fortified and inspired by his example—he too must take up his burden and stand alone in the loneliness of kingship. To both the King and Queen Mary every heart and mind will turn to-day with all the encouragement that sympathy and affection can give. But more than that can be done. In the spirit of King George the least of us can resolve to go on doing his best for his country in truth and justice ; and to do so is to stand beside the King himself, to lighten his burden and to strengthen his hand.

THE FUNERAL PROCESSION

THE MARCH FROM WESTMINSTER TO PADDINGTON

The Royal funeral procession left Westminster Hall for Paddington in the following order :

An officer of the Headquarter Staff—Major T. H. Massy-Beresford, M.C.

FIRST AND SECOND DIVISION OF ESCORT, Royal Horse Guards. Band of Third Carabiniers (Prince of Wales's Dragoon Guards). Band of Household Cavalry. Detachment of the Royal Air Force. Detachment of the London University Officers Training Corps.

Detachments from Dominion and Colonial Corps.
Colonial Corps. Dominion Air Force. Dominion Corps of Officers. Dominion Navy.

Detachments from Units of the Territorial Army of which His late Majesty was Colonel-in-Chief or Honorary Colonel.
3rd Battalion (Militia) The West Yorkshire Regiment (Prince of Wales's Own). 8th Battalion The Hampshire Regiment. The Duke of Lancaster's Own Yeomanry. 108th Field Brigade, Royal Artillery. Honourable Artillery Company. Indian Services.

Detachments from Regiments and Corps of the Regular Army of which His late Majesty was Colonel-in-Chief.
Royal Tank Corps.

Infantry of the Line.—The Royal Irish Fusiliers (Princess Victoria's). The Queen's Own Cameron Highlanders. The Manchester Regiment. The King's Royal Rifle Corps. The Black Watch (Royal Highland Regiment). The Royal Welch Fusiliers. The Royal Norfolk Regiment. The King's Regiment (Liverpool). The Royal Fusiliers (City of London Regiment). The King's Own Royal Regiment (Lancaster).

Foot Guards.—Welsh Guards. Irish Guards. Scots Guards. Coldstream Guards. Grenadier Guards. Corps of Royal Engineers. Royal Regiment of Artillery.

Cavalry of the Line.—1st The Royal Dragoons. 10th Royal Hussars (Prince o Wales's Own).

Household Cavalry.—Royal Horse Guards. The Life Guards.

Representative Detachments.—The Royal Marines. The Royal Navy.

Representative Officers of Foreign Navies, Armies and Air Forces, including Naval, Military, and Air Attachés.

Denmark.	*Afghanistan.*	*Hungary.*	*Rumania.*
Vice-Admiral Rechnitser.	General Mohomed Omer Khan.	Major-Gen. L. de Keresztes-Fischer.	Brig.-General Macici.

107

Mexico.
Captain E. V.
Zarco.

Yugoslavia.
Army General
Emilo Belitch.

Bulgaria.
Lt.-Col. Cyrille
Jantchouleff.

Greece.
Captain
Kawadias.

Lithuania.
Lt.-Gen. Tallat
Kelpsa.

Peru.
Commander
C. A. Gilardi.

Finland.
Commander Helger
Gröndahl.

Czechoslovakia.
Inspector-Gen.
Yan Syrovy.

Sweden.
Vice-Adm. C.
L. de Champs.

Austria.
Major-Gen.
T. Haselmayr.

Holland.
Major-Gen. Baron
van Voorst-Tot-Voorst.

Portugal.
General Vieira
da Rocha.

Chile.
Rear-Adm. Don
Calixto Rogers.

Poland.
Rear-Admiral
Unrug.

Turkey.
General
Fahrettin Altay.

France.
Admiral
Durand-Viel.

France.
General
Gamelin.

United States of America.
Captain
J. A. Furer.

Lt.-Colonel
Hayes A. Kroner.

Germany.
Admiral
Elbrecht.

Germany.
General
G. Von Runsted.

Soviet Union.
Marshal
Tukachevski.

Italy.
H.E. Admiral
Giuseppe Cantu.

General
Francesco Grazioli.

Argentine Republic.
Colonel Juan
Pierrestegui.

Spain.
General Don
Francisco Franco.

Japan.
Captain
Risaburo Fujita.

Colonel
Maruyama.

Belgium.
Lt.-General
Gillieaux.

Lt.-General
Van den Bergen.

Brazil.
Captain
Natal Arnaud.

Chaplains.

Rev. A. McHardy,
M.C., M.A.

Rev. J. Lynn,
B.A., D.D.,
Deputy
Chaplain-General to
the Forces.

Rev. E. H. Thorold,
C.B., C.B.E., M.A.,
D.D., K.H.C.,
Chaplain-General to
the Forces.

Rev. J. R. Walker,
M.A., K.H.C.,
Chaplain-in-Chief,
Royal Air Force.

Rev. T. Crick, M.V.O.,
M.A., K.H.C.,
Chaplain, Royal Navy.

Rt. Rev. Bishop J. Day,
D.S.O.

The Venerable Archdeacon
A. D. Gilbertson, O.B.E.,
M.A., K.H.C.

Air Ministry Staff.

Air Commodore
W. L. Welsh,
D.S.C., A.F.C.

Air Commodore
J. B. Bowen,
O.B.E.

Air Vice-Marshal
J. E. A. Baldwin,
D.S.O., O.B.E.,

Air Commodore
R. H. Verney,
O.B.E.

Air Officers Commanding and Commanding-in-Chief.

Air Commodore
J. C. Quinnell,
D.F.C.

Air Marshal
Sir Arthur H.
Longmore,
K.C.B., D.S.O.

Air Marshal
Sir John M.
Steel, K.C.B.,
K.B.E., C.M.G.,

Air Marshal
C. S. Burnett,
K.C.B., C.B.E.,
D.S.O.

Marshals of the Royal Air Force.

Sir John M. Salmond,
G.C.B., C.M.G., C.V.O., D.S.O.

The Viscount Trenchard,
G.C.B., G.C.V.O., D.S.O.

Air Council.

Air Marshal
Sir Cyril L. N. Newall,
K.C.B., C.M.G., C.B.E.

Air Marshal
F. W. Bowhill,
K.C.B., C.M.G., D.S.O.

Air Marshal
Sir Hugh C. T. Dowding,
K.C.B., C.M.G.

THE FUNERAL PROCESSION

Representative Colonels-Commandant and Colonels of His late Majesty's Regiments

Colonel H. M. Hardcastle, T.D.	Major-General Sir Ernest D. Swinton, K.B.E., C.B., D.S.O.	Major-General N. J. G. Cameron, C.B., C.M.G.	The Earl Fortescue, M.C.
Colonel F. H. Dorling, D.S.O.	Lieut.-General the Hon. Sir A. Richard Montagu- Stuart-Wortley, K.C.B., K.C.M.G., D.S.O.	Lieut.-General Sir R. F. C. Foster, K.C.B., C.M.G., D.S.O.	Major-General Sir Steuart Hare, K.C.M.G., C.B.
General St. G. B. Armstrong, C.B., C.M.G.	Major-General W. P. H. Hill, C.B., C.M.G., D.S.O.	Lieut.-General O. C. Borrett, C.B., C.M.G., C.B.E., D.S.O.	General Sir E. Peter Strickland, K.C.B., K.B.E., C.M.G., D.S.O.
Brig.-General the Viscount Hampden, G.C.V.O., K.C.B., C.M.G.	Lieut.-General Sir J. Ronald E. Charles, K.C.B., C.M.G., D.S.O.	Major-General E. H. Willis, C.B., C.M.G.	Brig.-General E. Makins, C.B., D.S.O.

General Officer Commanding.

Major-General W. J. N. Cooke-Collis, C.B., C.M.G., D.S.O.

General Officers Commanding-in-Chief.

Lieut.-General Sir Walter M. St. G. Kirke,
K.C.B., C.M.G., D.S.O.

Lieut.-General Sir Archibald R. Cameron
K.C.B., C.M.G.

Field-Marshals.

Sir Philip W. Chetwode, Bart., G.C.B., O.M., G.C.S.I., K.C.M.G., D.S.O.	The Lord Milne, G.C.B., G.C.M.G., D.S.O.	Sir Claud W. Jacob, G.C.B., G.C.S.I., K.C.M.G.	The Earl of Cavan, K.P., G.C.B., G.C.M.G., G.C.V.O., G.B.E.

Headquarters Staff of the Army.

Major-General B. A. Hill, D.S.O.	Major-General A. J. Hunter, C.B., C.M.G., D.S.O., M.C.	Lieut.-General Sir Charles Bonham-Carter, K.C.B., C.M.G., D.S.O.	Major-General A. E. McNamara, C.B., C.M.G., D.S.O.	Major-General W. K. Venning, C.B., C.M.G., C.B.E., M.C.

Army Council.

Lieut.-General Sir Hugh Elles, K.C.B., K.C.M.G., K.C.V.O., D.S.O.	Field-Marshal Sir Archibald Montgomery-Massingberd, G.C.B., K.C.M.G.	Lieut.-General Sir Reginald May, K.C.B., K.B.E., C.M.G., D.S.O.

Representatives of the Merchant Navy.

Thomas Goodwin, Esq., Chief Engineer.	Captain R. Harrison, D.S.O., R.D., R.N.R.	Captain Edward Holland.	Captain H. G. Cox.

*Two Captains of the Royal
Naval Volunteer Reserve.*

*Two Captains of the Royal
Naval Reserve.*

Admiralty Headquarters Staff.

Vice-Admiral G. C. Dickens, C.B., C.M.G.	Vice-Admiral S. R. Bailey, C.B., C.B.E., D.S.O.	Vice-Admiral R. M. Colvin, C.B., C.B.E.	Vice-Admiral Sir G. K. Chetwode, K.C.B., C.B.E.

Commanders-in-Chief, Royal Navy.

Vice-Admiral Sir Edward R. G. R. Evans, K.C.B., D.S.O.	Admiral the Hon. Sir R. A. R. Plunkett- Ernle-Erle-Drax, K.C.B., D.S.O.	Admiral the Earl of Cork and Orrery, G.C.V.O., K.C.B.

HAIL AND FAREWELL

Admirals of the Fleet.

Admiral of the Fleet Sir Reginald Tyrwhitt, Bart., G.C.B., D.S.O.

Admiral of the Fleet Sir Frederick Field, G.C.B., K.C.M.G.

Admiral of the Fleet Sir Roger B. Keyes, Bart., G.C.B., K.C.V.O., C.M.G., D.S.O.

Admiral of the Fleet Sir O. de B. Brock, G.C.B., K.C.M.G., K.C.V.O.

Admiral of the Fleet Sir H. F. Oliver, G.C.B., K.C.M.G., M.V.O.

Admiral of the Fleet The Earl Beatty, G.C.B., O.M., G.C.V.O., D.S.O.

Board of Admiralty.

Sir Oswyn A. R. Murray, G.C.B.

K. M. Lindsay, Esq., M.P.

Lord Stanley, M.C., M.P.

Rear-Admiral C. E. Kennedy-Purvis, C.B.

Vice-Admiral Sir W. M. James, K.C.B.

Vice-Admiral P. L. H. Noble, C.B., C.V.O.

Vice-Admiral Sir R. Henderson, K.C.B.

Admiral Sir M. E. Dunbar-Nasmith, V.C., K.C.B.

Admiral of the Fleet Sir Ernle Chatfield, G.C.B., K.C.M.G., C.V.O.

The Rt. Hon. the Viscount Monsell, G.B.E.

Aides-de-Camp to His late Majesty.

Group Captain R. Leckie, D.S.O., D.S.C., D.F.C.

Group Captain F. L. Robinson, D.S.O., M.C., D.F.C.

Group Captain R. M. Hill, M.C., A.F.C.

Colonel W. Anderson, D.S.O., M.C., T.D.

Colonel J. C. M. Doran, C.B.E., D.S.O.

Colonel (temp. Brig.) F. W. Bullock-Marsham, D.S.O., M.C.

Colonel (temp. Brig.) E. A. Beck, D.S.O.

Colonel G. J. Giffard, D.S.O.

Colonel (temp. Brig.) H. N. North, D.S.O.

Colonel (temp. Brig.) A. K. Main, D.S.O.

Colonel F. B. Hurndall, M.C.

Colonel A. E. Davidson, D.S.O.

Colonel R. L. McCall, D.S.O., M.C.

Colonel J. F. R. Hope, C.B.E., D.S.O.

Colonel G. F. Perkins, D.S.O.

Colonel C. R. Gillett, D.S.O.

Colonel A. G. L'E. Le Gallais, M.C.

Colonel (temp. Brig.) R. H. R. Benson, C.B.E.

Colonel (temp. Brig.) R. H. Willan, D.S.O., M.C.

Colonel P. L. Hanbury, C.M.G., D.S.O.

Brevet-Colonel T. C. Dunlop, T.D.

Colonel J. L. Jack, D.S.O.

Colonel E. C. M. Phillips, D.S.O., T.D.

Colonel J. B. McKaig, C.B., D.S.O., T.D.

Colonel E. J. King, C.M.G., T.D.

Colonel Sir Norman A. Orr Ewing, Bart., D.S.O.

Colonel S. W. L. Ashwanden, D.S.O., T.D.

Colonel R. W. Burnyeat, D.S.O., T.D.

Colonel C. H. Pank, C.M.G., D.S.O., T.D.

Colonel the Lord Vivian, D.S.O., T.D.

Colonel G. H. Stobart, C.B.E., D.S.O.

Major (Hon. Lieut.-Colonel) R. W. Randall.

Colonel D. S. Branson, D.S.O., M.C., T.D.

Colonel E. Treffry, C.M.G., O.B.E., T.D.

Colonel E. H. Eley, C.M.G., C.B.E., D.S.O.

Colonel L. Partridge, D.S.O., T.D.

Colonel F. H. Ballantine-Dykes, D.S.O., O.B.E.

Colonel F. G. Danielsen, D.S.O., T.D.

Colonel B. Abel Smith, D.S.O., M.C., T.D.

Colonel Sir Donald W. Cameron of Lochiel, K.T., C.M.G.

Colonel A. E. Williams, D.S.O.

Captain E. W. Swan, O.B.E., R.N.V.R.

Captain W. C. Tarrant, O.B.E., R.D., R.N.R.

Eng. Captain H. H. Perring.

Eng. Captain A. W. Le Page, D.S.O.

THE FUNERAL PROCESSION

Brigadier H. Blount, D.S.O., R.M.	Captain P. Macnamara.	Captain M. J. R. Maxwell-Scott, D.S.O.	Captain R. V. Holt, D.S.O., M.V.O.
Captain E. B. Cloete.		Captain K. D. W. Macpherson.	Brigadier J. W. Hudleston, C.B., R.M.

Principal Air Aide-de-Camp to His late Majesty.

Air Chief Marshal Sir Edward Ellington, G.C.B., C.M.G., C.B.E.

Aides-de-Camp General to His late Majesty.

General Sir John Burnett-Stuart, K.C.B., K.B.E., C.M.G., D.S.O.	General the Hon. Sir J. Francis Gathorne- Hardy, G.C.B., G.C.V.O., C.M.G., D.S.O.	General Sir Cyril Deverell, G.C.B., K.B.E.	General Sir Alexander Wardrop, K.C.B., C.M.G.

First and Principal Naval Aide-de-Camp to His late Majesty.

Admiral Sir John Kelly, G.C.B., G.C.V.O.

Band of the Royal Air Force.

Band of Royal Marines.

Massed Bands of the Brigade of Guards (less Band of Coldstream Guards).

Royal Engineers Band.

Royal Artillery Band.

Massed Pipers of The Queen's Own Cameron Highlanders.

The Black Watch (Royal Highland Regiment).

Irish Guards.

Scots Guards.

The Earl Marshal.

The Duke of Norfolk.

Captain of the Gentlemen-at-Arms. Brigadier-General the Earl of Lucan, K.B.E., C.B.	*Captain General of the King's Bodyguard for Scotland (Royal Company of Archers).* The Lord Elphinstone, K.T.	*Captain of the Yeomen of the Guard.* Colonel the Lord Templemore, D.S.O., O.B.E.

Rear-Admiral of the United Kingdom. Admiral Sir Montague Browning, G.C.B., G.C.M.G., G.C.V.O.	*Gold Stick in Waiting.* Field-Marshal Sir William R. Birdwood, Bart., G.C.B., G.C.S.I., G.C.M.G., C.I.E., D.S.O.	*Vice-Admiral of the United Kingdom.* Admiral the Hon. Sir Stanley Colville, G.C.B., G.C.M.G., G.C.V.O.

Treasurer of the Household. Sir George Penny, Bart., M.P.	*Comptroller of the Household.* Colonel Sir Lambert Ward, Bart., D.S.O., M.P.

The Master of the Horse. The Earl of Granard, K.P., G.C.V.O.	*The Lord Steward.* The Earl of Shaftesbury, K.P., G.C.V.O., C.B.E.

His late Majesty's Valet. Mr. W. Crisp.	*His late Majesty's Valet.* Mr. S. J. Miller.

Sergeant Footman. Mr. T. Tubb.	*Superintendent of His late Majesty's Wardrobe* Mr. R. Howlett.

III

Extra Equerries to
His late Majesty.

Col. the Hon. Sir
George Crichton,
G.C.V.O.

Bearer Party, King's Company, Grenadier Guards.

Naval Gun's Crew under the command of Captain A. L. St. G. Lyster, R.N.

Bearer Party, King's Company, Grenadier Guards.

Extra Equerries to
His late Majesty.

Major Sir Edward
Seymour,
K.C.V.O., D.S.O.,
O.B.E.

Admiral the Hon.
Sir Herbert
Meade-
Fetherstonhaugh,
G.C.V.O., C.B.,
D.S.O.

Gentlemen at Arms and Yeomen of the Guard.

Brigadier Henry
Tomkinson,
D.S.O.

Gentlemen at Arms and Yeomen of the Guard.

Admiral
[Sir Henry Buller,
G.C.V.O., C.B.

Equerries to His
late Majesty.

Brig.-Gen.
George Paynter,
C.M.G., C.V.O.,
D.S.O.

Lt.-Col. Lord
Alastair
Innes-Ker,
C.V.O., D.S.O.
Major the Hon.
Alexander
Hardinge,
C.B., C.V.O.,
M.C.

Equerries to His
late Majesty.

Captain Lord
Claud
Hamilton,
C.M.G.,
C.V.O., D.S.O.
Lt.-Col. Sir
Reginald
Seymour,
K.C.V.O.

Admiral the Hon.
Sir Hubert
Brand, G.C.B.,
K.C.M.G.,
K.C.V.O.

Gun Carriage.

Major-Gen. Sir
Harry Watson,
K.B.E., C.B., C.M.G.,
C.I.E., M.V.O.

Col. the Lord
Wigram,
G.C.B.,
G.C.V.O.,
C.S.I.

Captain Sir
Bryan Godfrey-
Faussett,
G.C.V.O.,
C.M.G., R.N.

Colonel Sir Henry
Streatfeild,
G.C.V.O., C.B.,
C.M.G.

Second in command of Escort.

Officer commanding Escort.
Trumpeter.

Royal Standard.

Adjutant-General to the Forces.
Lt.-Gen. Sir Harry H. S. Knox,
K.C.B., D.S.O.

borne by a Warrant Officer of the Household Cavalry.

HIS MAJESTY
THE KING.

His Royal Highness
The Duke of Kent, K.G.

His Royal Highness
The Duke of York, K.G.

His Royal Highness
The Duke of Gloucester, K.G.

Field-Officer-in-Brigade-Waiting.
Lt.-Col. W. A. F. L. Fox-Pitt,
M.C. (Welsh Guards).

Silver-Stick in Waiting.
Lt.-Col. F. B. de Klée
(Royal Horse Guards).

The Earl of
Athlone, K.G.

H.R.H. The Crown
Prince of Norway.

His Majesty The
King of Norway.

The Earl of
Harewood, K.G.

King Edward VIII and his brothers in the procession through London.

THE FUNERAL PROCESSION

The President of the French Republic.

His Majesty The King of Denmark and Iceland.

His Majesty The King of Rumania.

His Majesty The King of the Bulgarians.

His Majesty The King of the Belgians.

H.R.H. The Crown Prince of Sweden.

H.R.H. The Prince Regent of Yugoslavia.

H.R.H. The Prince of Piedmont.

H.R.H. The Prince of Said.

H.R.H. The Crown Prince of Greece.

H.R.H. Monseigneur Prince Felix of Luxemburg.

H.R.H. The Prince Zeid.

H.R.H. Prince Chula Chakradongse.

H.R.H. Prince Axel of Denmark.

H.R.H. The Duke of Saxe-Coburg and Gotha.

The Hereditary Grand Duke of Hesse.

H.R.H. Duc de Némours.

H.R.H. Prince George of Greece.

H.R.H. Prince Nicholas of Greece.

Prince Ernst August of Brunswick.

H.R.H. The Count of Flanders.

Prince Frederick of Prussia.

H.R.H. The Duke of Braganza.

H.R.H. The Infante Alfonso of Spain.

H.R.H. Prince Alvaro of Orleans-Bourbon.

The Grand Duke Dimitri of Russia.

Prince Salih.

The Marquess of Carisbrooke, G.C.B., G.C.V.O.

His Royal Highness
The Prince Arthur of Connaught, K.G.
(representing His Royal Highness
The Duke of Connaught).

Lord Louis Mountbatten, K.C.V.O.

Earl of Macduff.

The Marquess of Milford Haven, G.C.V.O.

Lord Carnegie, K.C.V.O.

The Marquess of Cambridge, G.C.V.O.

Lord Frederick Cambridge.

Alexander Ramsay, Esq.

The Duke of Beaufort, G.C.V.O.

Major Henry Abel Smith.

CARRIAGE

(*Glass Coach with pair of Bay Horses*).

HER MAJESTY QUEEN MARY.

Her Majesty Queen Maud of Norway.

Her Royal Highness the Princess Royal.

Her Royal Highness the Duchess of York.

Private Secretary to Her Majesty Queen Mary.
The Hon. Gerald Chichester, C.V.O.

Lord Chamberlain to Her Majesty Queen Mary.
The Marquess of Anglesey, G.C.V.O.

Excmo Senor Don Joaquin Urzaiz.

H.E. Senhor Regis De Oliveira.

H.E. Mr. Sato.

Freiherr von Neurath.

Monsieur Le Breton.

Monsieur Litvinoff.

H.E. General Sosnkowski.

Mr. Norman Davis.

Dr. T. R. Aras.

H.E. Dr. Montero.

H.E. Mr. Quo Tai-chi.

H.E. Senor Don Agustin Edwards.

Prince Ernst Rudiger Starhemberg.

Vice-Admiral Jonkheer G. L. Schorer.

Monsieur Paravicini.

Field-Marshal Baron Karl Mannerheim.

Monsieur Masaryk.

Sheikh Hafiz Wahba.

H.E. Faiz Mohammed Khan.

Monsieur Margers Skujenieks.

Senor Don Alfredo Benavides.

Monsieur Hussein Ala.

Don Alberto Dodero

Monsieur S. Lozorsitis.

Senor Dr. Don Maximiliano Henriquez-Urena.

Gen. Laidoner.

Lt.-Gen. Krishna Shumsher Jung Bahadur Rana.

113

I

HAIL AND FAREWELL

Senor Don Simon Patino. Monsieur Bassols. Dr. Petro Martinez Fraga.
Conte de Maleville. Monsieur Kalman de Kanya H.E. Enrico Garda.

Major His Highness the Raja of His Highness the Maharajah of
Sawantwadi, K.C.S.I. Dhrangadhra, G.C.I.E., K.C.S.I.

The High Commissioner for the *The High Commissioner*
Commonwealth of Australia. *for the Dominion of Canada.*

The Right Hon. S. M. Bruce, C.H., M.C. The Hon. Vincent Massey.

The High Commissioner for the Union *The High Commissioner for the Dominion*
of South Africa. *of New Zealand.*

C. te Water, Esq. The Hon. Sir James Parr, G.C.M.G.

The High Commissioner for *The High Commissioner for the*
Southern Rhodesia. *Irish Free State.*

S. M. L. O'Keeffe, Esq., C.M.G. J. W. Dulanty, Esq., C.B., C.B.E.

Lieut. C. G. V. Tryon *Crown Equerry,* Captain R. E. Laycock
(Grenadier Guards), Col. Sir Arthur E. (Royal Horse Guards),
Adjutant-in-Brigade Waiting. Erskine, G.C.V.O., D.S.O. Silver Stick Adjutant.

FIRST CARRIAGE.
(Glass Coach and pair of Bay Horses.)

H.M. The Queen Victoria Eugénie. H.R.H. The Duchess of Gloucester.
H.R.H. The Duchess of Kent. H.R.H. The Princess Arthur of Connaught.

SECOND CARRIAGE.
(State Landau and pair of Bay Horses.)

H.R.H. The Princess Alice, Countess of Lady Maud Carnegie.
Athlone. Lady Patricia Ramsay.
H.R.H. The Infanta Beatrice of Spain.

THIRD CARRIAGE.
(State Landau and pair of Bay Horses.)

H.R.H. The Crown Princess of Denmark. H.R.H. The Crown Princess of Sweden.
H.R.H. The Duchess of Saxe-Coburg The Dowager Marchioness of Milford
and Gotha. Haven.

FOURTH CARRIAGE.
(State Landau and pair of Bay Horses.)

H.H. The Princess Helena Victoria. H.H. The Princess Marie Louise.
The Duchess of Beaufort. The Marchioness of Milford Haven.

FIFTH CARRIAGE.
(State Landau and pair of Bay Horses.)

Lady May Abel Smith. Lady Helena Gibbs.
Viscount Lascelles. Hon. Gerald Lascelles.

SIXTH CARRIAGE.
(State Landau and pair of Bay Horses.)

The Marchioness of Cambridge. Lady Iris Mountbatten.
Lady Mary Cambridge.

SEVENTH CARRIAGE.
(State Landau and pair of Bay Horses.)

The Mistress of the Robes. The Lady in Waiting.
The Woman of the Bedchamber. Miss von Hanno.

THE FUNERAL PROCESSION

Household of His late Majesty.

The Earl of Dunmore, V.C., D.S.O.,
M.V.O.

The Earl of Feversham.

Lords in Waiting.

Brig.-General the Viscount Hampden,
G.C.V.O., K.C.B., C.M.G.

The Viscount Gage.　　　The Earl of Munster.

Financial Secretary.

Sir Ralph Harwood, K.C.B., K.C.V.O., C.B.E.

Surgeon-Apothecary
at Sandringham.

Sir Frederic Willans,
K.C.V.O.

Physician in Ordinary.

The Lord Dawson of Penn,
G.C.V.O., K.C.B., K.C.M.G.

Surgeon-Apothecary.

Sir Stanley Hewett, K.C.B.,
K.C.V.O., K.B.E.

Grooms in Waiting.

Col. Sir Victor Mackenzie,
Bart., D.S.O., M.V.O.

Major Sir Philip Hunloke,
K.C.V.O.

Major the Hon. Sir Richard
Molyneux, C.V.O.

Assistant Private Secretary.

Alan Lascelles, Esq., C.M.G.,
M.V.O., M.C.

Assistant Private Secretary and
Secretary of the Order of the Garter.

Frank Mitchell, Esq., C.V.O., C.B.E.

Assistant Comptroller, Lord
Chamberlain's Department.

Major Colin Gordon, C.V.O.

Deputy Master of the Household.

Brig.-Gen. Sir Hill Child, Bart.,
C.B., C.M.G., C.V.O., D.S.O.

Gentlemen Ushers.

Brig.-Gen. Gerald
Trotter, C.B.,
C.M.G., C.V.O.,
C.B.E., D.S.O.

Capt. Charles Irvine,
M.V.O., O.B.E.

The Hon. Sir
Montague Eliot,
K.C.V.O., O.B.E.

Admiral Philip
Nelson-Ward,
M.V.O.

John Hanbury-
Williams, Esq.

Captain
Humphrey Lloyd,
M.V.O., M.C.

Wing Commander
Sir Louis Greig,
K.B.E., C.V.O.

Colonel the Hon.
George Herbert,
T.D.

Lt.-Colonel
Frederick
Packe.

Major
John Wickham,
M.V.O.

Equerry.

Major Sir John Aird,
Bart., M.C.

Admiral Sir Lionel
Halsey, G.C.M.G.,
G.C.V.O., K.C.I.E., C.B.

Equerry.

Lt.-Col. the Hon. Piers Legh,
M.V.O., O.B.E.

Equerry to H.R.H. the
Duke of Kent.

Maj. Humphrey Butler,
M.V.O., M.C.

Equerry to H.R.H. the
Duke of York.

Rear-Adm. Sir Basil
Brooke, K.C.V.O.

Comptroller to H.R.H. the
Duke of Gloucester.

Maj. Ronald
Stanyforth, M.V.O.

SUITES OF FOREIGN ROYALTIES AND ENGLISH SUITES ATTACHED

NORWAY.—An Equerry. Lord Colebrooke. Captain Sir B. Godfrey-Faussett.

DENMARK.—Colonel C. C. B. Dreyer. Brig.-Gen. Viscount Hampden. Major John
Wickham.

RUMANIA.—General Baliff. General Iliasevici. The Earl of Munster.

FRANCE.—Monsieur Magre. Monsieur de Fouquières. General Braconnier. Admiral
Bigot. Viscount Gage. Sir W. Erskine.

BELGIUM.—M. le Comte Louis Cornet de Ways Ruart. The Earl of Dunmore. Lt.-Col. F. Packe.

BULGARIA.—Two Aides-de-Camp. The Earl of Feversham.

YUGOSLAVIA.—Monsieur Antitch. General Tcholak-Antitch. Major The Hon. Sir R. Molyneux.

ITALY.—H. E. General Adlo Aymonino. Brigadier-General Giulio Marinetti. Count di Sant'Elia. Sir Ronald Graham.

SWEDEN.—Monsieur N. de Rudebeck. Admiral The Hon. Sir H. Meade-Fetherstonhaugh.

GREECE.—Major Levidis. Captain Vandoros. Sir Philip Hunloke.

EGYPT.—H.E. Mahmoud Fakhry Pacha.

IRAQ.—Sir F. Humphreys.

SIAM.—Captain Rona Bhakas. Captain the Hon. Ivan Hay.

LUXEMBURG.—Colonel the Hon. George Herbert.

GERMANY.—Major Drage. Sir H. Rumbold. Brigadier-General G. Paynter.

SPAIN.—Sir Montague Eliot.

ALBANIA.—Wing Commander Sir Louis Greig.

MEMBERS OF FOREIGN GOVERNMENTS
OTHER MEMBERS OF FOREIGN DELEGATIONS AND ENGLISH SUITES ATTACHED

BELGIUM.—Monsieur Van Zeeland, Prime Minister and Minister of Foreign Affairs. Monsieur Devèze, Minister of Defence.

FRANCE.—Monsieur Flandin, Minister of Foreign Affairs. Monsieur Pietrie, Minister of Marine. Marshal Pétain. Monsieur Jean Chiappe, Président du Conseil Municipal de Paris.

POLAND.—Monsieur Skirmunt.

PORTUGAL.—H.E. Col. A. Valdez de Passos e Sousa, Minister for War. H.E. Commander M. O. Bettencourt, Minister for Marine.

YUGOSLAVIA.—Monsieur Ljubomir Tomashitch, President of the Senate.

RUMANIA.—Monsieur N. Titulescu, Minister of Foreign Affairs. Monsieur A. Lapedatu, Minister of Fine Arts. General Paul Anghelescu, Minister of Defence.

ALBANIA.—H.E. Dr. Faud Aslani.

BELGIUM.—Conte Adrian van der Burch. Sir R. Sperling.

JAPAN.—Sir Victor Wellesley.

SPAIN.—Sir George Mounsey.

ARGENTINE.—R. L. Craigie, Esq.

SOVIET UNION.—Sir Ronald Macleay.

UNITED STATES.—Lord Howard of Penrith.

TURKEY.—Sir William Max-Muller.

POLAND.—General Sir G. Jeffreys.

PORTUGAL.—Sir Stephen Gazelee.

NETHERLANDS.—Admiral Sir H. Buller.

AUSTRIA.—O. G. Sargent, Esq.

FINLAND.—Major-General Sir George MacDonogh.

AFGHANISTAN.—Sir L. Oliphant.

URUGUAY.—J. M. Troutbeck, Esq.

LITHUANIA.—L. Collier, Esq.

ESTONIA.—Captain I. D. Brown.

RUMANIA.—Sir Malcolm Robertson.

HUNGARY.—Colonel Sir Victor Mackenzie, Bart.

BRAZIL.—Senhor Carlos Taylor. Captain Natal Arnaud.

BELGIUM.—Monsieur le Lt.-Gen. Tilkens. Monsieur le Commandant van den Huevel. Monsieur le Capitaine Baron Jacques de Dixmude. Le Commandant Baron Goffinet. Monsieur le Vicomte de Lantsheere. Monsieur le Capitaine de Rossius d'Humain. Vicomte du Parc. Comte Eugene de Grunne. Captain Gerald Ellis.

JAPAN.—Mr. K. Miyazaki. Mr. A. Matsui. Captain R. L. Burnett, R.N. Colonel R. C. Bingham.

SPAIN.—Lieut.-Col. Franco. Rear-Admiral Gervera. Adjutant of Rear-Admiral. Lieut.-Col. Nevado. Captain Martinez. H.E. Senor Don Manuel Travesado. Senor Don Luis Soller. Senor Don Luis Torres Quevado.

ARGENTINE REPULIC.—Senhor Don Carlos Miguens. Senhor Dr. Echague. Senhor Dr. Barrenechea. Captain Mario Fincati.

ITALY.—Lieut.-Col. Giuseppe Leonardi. Captain Mario Grandi. Lieutenant Eliso Porta. Colonel H. R. Stevens.

SOVIET UNION.—Major E. C. Hay.

GERMANY.—General Kaupisch. Herr Von Kotze. Herr Von Etsdorf. Major Kitschmann. Ober Lieutenant Schultz. Colonel von Kotze. Colonel B. C. Paget.

UNITED STATES OF AMERICA.—Lieut.-Colonel Raymond Lee. Captain Wallis Anderson. Captain McNamara, R.N. Captain C. Irvine.

FRANCE.—Colonel Marceau. Monsieur Fouries. Monsieur Gaillard. Monsieur Bucaille. Monsieur Jean de Castellane. Monsieur des Isnards. Monsieur Boissiere. Monsieur Marron. Captain M. P. Berkeley.

TURKEY.—Bay Nuri Conker. General Salih. Captain de Vaisseau Sait Halman. Lt.-Col. Celâl. Major Celâl. Admiral Sir Percy Grant. Captain L. Watkinson.

POLAND.—Monsieur Switalski. Commander Solski. Colonel Trzaska-Durski. Captain Masielewicz. J. L. Dodds, Esq. Lt. D. Lennox-Boyd.

CHILE.—Colonel Don H. Luco. Commander F. Beduneau. Senor Don H. Phillips. Senor Don Louis Renard. Senor Dr. Don Manuel-Pereira.

PORTUGAL.—H.E. Dr. A. D'Oliveira. Admiral Oliveira Kuzauty. Two Aides-de-Camp Vice-Admiral A. J. Davies. Mr. R. Grant Watson.

NETHERLANDS.—Lieut.-Colonel Jonkheer van Ellemeet. Lieutenant Jonkheer van Lawick. Colonel R. Leatham.

AUSTRIA.—Herr K. von Zeileissen. Prince F. Windisch-Graetz. Colonel F. G. Whitefoord.

SWEDEN.—Major B. de Uggla.

CZECHOSLOVAKIA.—Colonel Vaclav Kalina. General Serge Vojcechovsky.

FINLAND.—Major Rosenbroijer. Lieut.-Colonel O. W. H. Leese.

AFGHANISTAN.—H.E. Sultan Ahmud Khan.

LITHUANIA.—Major M. C. Brownjohn.

IRAN.—H.E. A. A. Zarinkafsche. Mr. G. A. Ardalan. Mr. H. Zandjani.

EGYPT.—H.E. Ahmed Mohammed Hassanein Bey. Lieut.-Colonel Omar Fathi Bey. Captain S. B. Rawlins.

GREECE.—Commander Cortessis. Lieut.-Commander Constantinidis. Captain Cunninghame-Graham.

BULGARIA.—Captain Ross.

YUGOSLAVIA.—Senator Bogdan Gavrilovitch. Senator Albert Kramer. Monsieur J. Drashkovitch. General Emil Belitch. Colonel George Glischitch. Naval Captain Ermin Pavitch. Dimitrye Vouitch. Milovan Pinterovitch. Voislav Gatchinovitch. Josip Rogitch. Tchaslav Nikitovitch. Karel Gajchek. Dragomir Stoyadinovitch.

MEXICO.—F. Ashton Gwatkin, Esq.

CUBA.—Senor J. M. Lara. Senor J. E. Meyer. M. Peterson, Esq.

BOLIVIA.—Mr. Linares.

RUMANIA.—Monsieur E. Urdareanu. Colonel E. Zwiedeneck. Capt. Fundatzianu. Major M. Mihailescu. Colonel Palangeanu. Lieut.-Colonel Tenescu. Monsieur Golovan. Major-General S. S. Butler.

ALBANIA.—Group Commander Ndoc Kurti. O. O'Malley, Esq.

HUNGARY.—Count Stephen Czaky. Howard Smith, Esq.

LUXEMBURG.—Monsieur Collart. Captain Muller. D. J. Scott, Esq.

MONACO.—An Aide-de-Camp. H. J. Seymour, Esq.

Delegations of Officers of Foreign Armies, Navies and Air Services and Foreign Military Naval and Air Attachés.

BELGIUM.—Lieut.-General Tilkens, A.D.C. to the King of the Belgians. Lieut.-Genera Baron Vincotte (Military Attaché). Capt.-Commandant Hemeleers-Shenley (Assistant Military Attaché). Major L. F. E. Wouters, M.C. (Air Attaché). Commandant Goffinet. Captain de Rossius d'Humain.

JAPAN.—Major Y. Arisue (Assistant Military Attaché).

SPAIN.—Lieut.-Colonel Sr. Nevado. Lieut.-Colonel Franco. Captain Don Manuel Medina (Military and Naval Attaché). Captain Sr. Martinez. Commandant Antonio Barroso.

ARGENTINE REPUBLIC.—Capitán de Navio Don Mario Fincati (Naval Attaché).

ITALY.—General Marinetti Conti di Sant Elia, Div.-General Aimonino. Colonel Leonarde. Capitano di Fregata Conte Ferrante Capponi (Naval Attaché). Colonel Umberto Mondadori (Military Attaché). Major F. Marigliano (Assistant Military Attaché). Colonel A. Calderara (Air Attaché). Captain Grandi.

SOVIET UNION.—General V. K. Putna (Military and Air Attaché). Colonel G. Gervassy (Assistant Air Attaché).

GERMANY.—Major-General Freiherr Geyr von Schweppenburg (Military Attaché) Captain E. Wassner (Naval Attaché). Colonel R. Wenninger (Air Attaché).

UNITED STATES OF AMERICA.—Commander W. Du Puy Baker (Assistant Naval Attaché). Lieut.-Commander L. C. Stevens (Assistant Naval Attaché). Lieutenant E. B. Strauss (Assistant Naval Attaché).

FRANCE.—Marshal Pétain and one Aide-de-Camp. General R. Voruz (Military Attaché). Lieut.-Colonel J. Cuny (Assistant Military Attaché). Capitaine de Frégate du Tour (Naval Attaché). Capitaine de Corvette V. A. M. Albertas (Air Attaché).

TURKEY.—Kor General Salih Omurtak. Major Jelal Unar (Minister for Foreign Affairs)

POLAND.—General Sosnkowski, Army Inspector.

CHILE.—Commander Don Francisco Beduneau (Naval Attaché).

PORTUGAL.—Colonel Passos e Sousa (Minister for War). Captain Jose Antonio Morais. Captain Sousa Mergulho. Lieutenant Madureira Proenca.

HOLLAND.—Colonel Jonkheer de Jonge Van Ellemeet. Lieutenant Jonkheer Van Lawick Van Pabst.

AUSTRIA.—Colonel Justus Jahn Von Jahnau (Military Attaché).

SWEDEN.—Commander G. Boldt-Christmas (Naval Attaché). Captain A. G. Ljungdahl (Military Attaché). Lieutenant H. Gisle (Assistant Military Attaché).

CZECHOSLOVAKIA.—Army General Sergej Vojcechovsky. Colonel Mrazek. Lieut.-Colonel Vacvlav Kalina (Military and Air Attaché). Squadron Leader Alois Kubita.

FINLAND.—Field-Marshal Baron Mannerheim, President of Council of National Defence.

The King of Norway, the Crown Prince of Norway, the Earl of Athlone, the
King of Rumania, the King of Denmark, M. Lebrun, the King of the Belgians,
and the King of Bulgaria in the procession to Windsor Castle.

Representatives of many foreign countries walking from Westminster Hall to
Paddington.

ESTONIA.—Lieut.-General Laidonner, K.C.M.G. (Commander-in-Chief, Estonian Army).

GREECE.—Major Levidis. Captain Vandoros (Royal Navy). Three Naval Officers.

YUGOSLAVIA.—Capitaine de Vaissfav Arnin Pavitch (Chief of Naval Staff). Air Force Colonel Dushan Radovitch.

RUMANIA.—General Anchelescu (War Minister). General Balif (Reserve of Officers). General Ilafievici. Colonel Zwiebeneck. Commander Funpapzeanu. Colonel Balalgealu. Lieut.-Colonel Pzelescu. Major Mihailescu. Lieut.-Colonel Urbareanu. Captain G. St. Dumitrescu (Military and Naval Attaché). Captain Cezar Marinescu (Assistant Military Attaché). Lieut.-Colonel E. Gheorghiu (Air Attaché).

HUNGARY.—Lieut.-Colonel Zoltan de Algya-Pap (Military Attaché).

THIRD DIVISION OF ESCORT, Royal Horse Guards.

Police Contingents.

Sir Charles G. Wickham, D.S.O., Inspector General, Royal Ulster Constabulary.

Colonel the Hon. Maurice Drummond, C.M.G., D.S.O., Deputy Commissioner of Police of the Metropolis.

Lieut.-Colonel Sir Hugh Turnbull, K.B.E., Commissioner of Police of the City of London.

Chief Inspector F. H. Durham, Metropolitan Police Force.

A detachment from the Metropolitan Police Force.

Inspector H. Sharp, City of London Police Force.

A detachment from the City of London Police Force.

Captain S. H. Van Neck, M.C., Chief Constable of Norfolk.

Superintendent E. Callaway (Buckinghamshire Constabulary).

Superintendent and Deputy Chief Constable W. Trigg, M.B.E. (Lincolnshire Constabulary).

A detachment from the County Police Forces of England and Wales, consisting of one representative of each force.

Mr. W. H. Smith, Chief Constable of Eastbourne Borough Police Force.

Superintendent J. E. Crofts, M.B.E. (Wolverhampton Borough Police Force).

Superintendent W. J. Lee (Plymouth City Police Force).

A detachment from the City and Borough Police Forces of England and Wales, consisting of one representative of each force.

J. Gauld, Esq., O.B.E., Chief Constable of Aberdeenshire.

Superintendent W. Rae, M.B.E. (Edinburgh City Police Force).

Superintendent A. Aitken (Lanarkshire Constabulary).

A detachment from the Scottish County, City and Burgh Police Forces, consisting of one representative of each force.

H. Connor, Esq., County Inspector, Royal Ulster Constabulary.

A detachment from the Royal Ulster Constabulary.

Fire Brigade Contingent.

Major C. B. Morris, M.C., Chief Officer, London Fire Brigade.

Lieutenant J. Fordham, R.N., Assistant Divisional Officer, London Fire Brigade.

A detachment from the London Fire Brigade.

FOURTH DIVISION OF ESCORT, Royal Horse Guards.

Seventy Minute Guns were fired while the Procession moved from Westminster Hall to Paddington Station.

On arrival at Paddington Station the Coffin was taken from the Gun Carriage by the Bearer Party of the Brigade of Guards and placed in the Royal Train, which conveyed The King and the other Royal Personages to Windsor.

ORDER OF PROCESSION AT WINDSOR

The funeral procession of King George from Windsor Station to St. George's Chapel varied in some details from the procession through London. Immediately after the Life Guards the four Pursuivants of Arms walked in front of the representative foreign officers. The other principal changes were contained in the programme of the part of the procession immediately preceding and surrounding the gun carriage, which is reproduced here for purposes of record :

SECOND DIVISION OF ESCORT, The Life Guards.

The Bands of
The Coldstream Guards,
The Life Guards.

Pipers of
The Black Watch (Royal Highland Regiment),
The Scots Guards.

York Herald.	*Windsor Herald.*
A. J. Toppin, Esq.	A. T. Butler, Esq., M.C.
Richmond Herald.	*Chester Herald.*
H. R. C. Martin, Esq.	J. D. Heaton-Armstrong, Esq.
Somerset Herald.	*Lancaster Herald.*
The Hon. G. R. Bellew, M.V.O.	A. G. B. Russell, Esq., M.V.O.
Norroy King of Arms.	*Clarenceux King of Arms.*
A. H. S. Howard, Esq., C.V.O.	A. W. S. Cochrane, Esq., C.V.O.
Ulster King of Arms.	*Lyon King of Arms.*
Major Sir N. R. Wilkinson, K.C.V.O.	Sir F. J. Grant, K.C.V.O.
Gentleman Usher of the Black Rod.	*Garter King of Arms.*
Lieut.-Gen. Sir William P. Pulteney, G.C.V.O., K.C.B., K.C.M.G., D.S.O.	Sir G. W. Wollaston, K.C.V.O.

The Earl Marshal.
The Duke of Norfolk.

Captain of the Gentlemen at Arms.	*Captain General of The King's Bodyguard for Scotland (Royal Company of Archers).*	*Captain of the Yeomen of the Guard.*
Brigadier-General The Earl of Lucan, K.B.E., C.B.	The Lord Elphinstone, K.T.	Colonel the Lord Templemore, D.S.O., O.B.E.

Treasurer of the Household.	*Comptroller of the Household.*
Sir George Penny, Bart., M.P.	Colonel Sir Lambert Ward, Bart., D.S.O., M.P.
The Master of the Horse.	*The Lord Steward.*
The Earl of Granard, K.P., G.C.V.O.	The Earl of Shaftesbury, K.P., G.C.V.O., C.B.E.
His late Majesty's Valet.	*His late Majesty's Valet.*
Mr. W. Crisp.	Mr. S. J. Miller.
Sergeant Footman.	*Superintendent of His late Majesty's Wardrobe.*
Mr. T. Tubb.	Mr. R. Howlett.

The King's Company Colour, borne by an Officer of the King's Company,
Grenadier Guards.

Extra Equerries to
His late Majesty.

Col. the Hon. Sir
George Crichton,
G.C.V.O.

Maj.-Gen. Sir
John Hanbury-
Williams,
G.C.V.O.,
K.C.B., C.M.G.

King's Company, Grenadier Guards.

Naval Gun's Crew under the
Command of Captain A. J. Power, R.N.

King's Company, Grenadier Guards.

Extra Equerries to
His late Majesty.

Major Sir Edward
Seymour,
K.C.V.O.,   D.S.O.,
O.B.E.

Admiral the Hon.
Sir Herbert
Meade-
Fetherstonhaugh,
G.C.V.O., C.B.,
D.S.O.

Brigadier Henry
Tomkinson,
D.S.O.

Admiral
Sir Henry Buller,
G.C.V.O., C.B.

Admiral the Hon.
Sir Hubert
Brand, G.C.B.,
K.C.M.G.,
K.C.V.O.

Major-Gen. Sir
Harry Watson,
K.B.E., C.B.,
C.M.G., C.I.E.,
M.V.O.

Equerries to His
late Majesty.

Lt.-Col. Lord
Alastair
Innes-Ker,
C.V.O., D.S.O.

Major the Hon.
Alexander
Hardinge,
C.B., C.V.O., M.C.

Col. the Lord
Wigram, G.C.B.,
G.C.V.O., C.S.I.

Gun Carriage.

Equerries to His
late Majesty.
Captain Lord
Claud Hamilton,
C.M.G., C.V.O.,
D.S.O.

Lt.-Col. Sir
Reginald
Seymour,
K.C.V.O.

Captain Sir Bryan
Godfrey-Faussett,
G.C.V.O., C.M.G.,
R.N.

Brig.-Gen.
George Paynter,
C.M.G., C.V.O.,
D.S.O.

Admiral
Sir Colin Keppel,
G.C.V.O.,
K.C.I.E., C.B.,
D.S.O.

Colonel Sir Henry
Streatfeild,
G.C.V.O., C.B.,
C.M.G.

Second in command of Escort.   Officer commanding Escort.

Royal
Standard.

Trumpeter.

Adjutant-General to the Forces.
Lt.-Gen. Sir Harry H. S. Knox
K.C.B., D.S.O.

borne by a Warrant Officer of the Household Cavalry.

HIS MAJESTY THE KING.

His Royal Highness
The Duke of Kent, K.G.

His Royal Highness
The Duke of York, K.G.

His Royal Highness
The Duke of Gloucester, K.G

Field-Officer-in-Brigade-Waiting.
Lt.-Col. W. A. F. L. Fox-Pitt, M.C.
(Welsh Guards).

Silver Stick in Waiting.
Lt.-Col. F. B. de Klée
(Royal Horse Guards).

CHAPTER V

JUDICAT ORBIS

THE tributes to King George as man and monarch, whether spoken or written, whether delivered at home, in the Empire or abroad, are beyond the compass of a single volume; here a selection must suffice. To this a fitting introduction is found in a leading article, bearing the title of this chapter, from *The Times* of Thursday, January 30 :

Time and tide do not wait upon mourners, and, as the insistent cares of everyday life resume their sway over the forefront of men's minds, the solemnities of King George's death and burial must be allowed to fade into history with other sorrows of the past. Yet it is not possible to turn away from the sad commemorations of these days without some acknowledgment of the consolation that has been felt by the people of the United Kingdom—whose loss is the more heavy as their privilege of near neighbourhood to the King was greater—because of the unanimity with which their grief has been shared by their fellow-subjects beyond the seas, and by many others who are not of their allegiance. During the hours of the funeral all the earth was in mourning. More than thirty national systems relayed the ceremony broadcast from Windsor, and the Two Minutes Silence travelled with the midday sun round the globe. The heads of many nations were present at the graveside; all sent personages of high degree to walk behind the King's body; but this was by no means the end of their tribute. In their own countries all peoples and languages united with us in reverence for the dead, and even the barriers that political estrangement has raised were as if they had never been when the common human impulse insisted on paying homage to one whose life had done honour to universal human nature.

Throughout the British Empire the people stood in spirit beside their brethren of the Mother Country. In the high summer of Australia 50,000 people assembled for an open-air service at Melbourne, where the largest of many wreaths was delivered by a body of Italians with the Fascist salute. Japanese, Chinese, and aboriginals joined in the service at Darwin, and the silence was observed by bathers at Sydney, standing to attention in the sea. Congregations in New Zealand called for additional services beyond those appointed. Dutch and English worshipped together in South Africa, and on the Rand black miners and white ceased work, thousands of feet below ground, as the procession left Westminster Hall. In Canada guns were hauled through the snow to the top of Mount Royal to salute the dead King, and in Newfoundland thousands walked through a blizzard to attend the services. India honoured the King-Emperor with the ceremonial of her many races, religions, and tongues ; while the Viceroy paid his tribute in Delhi, the people assembled for the same purpose in churches, mosques, and temples ; trains were stopped for five minutes through the length and breadth of the sub-continent ; Bombay expressed its grief by a *hartal*, or day of solemn mourning, the most complete of modern times ; and even the sacred pools of the Godavari River at Nasik were deserted by their pious bathers. Far removed in place and character, but one in sentiment, Bulawayo kept another day of mourning, in which Europeans and natives shared their observances. The English in Kenya went on pilgrimage to a hillside outside Nairobi, and there fashioned a vast crown of stone and flowers, as their ancestors, immemorial ages since, outlined the White Horse on the English hills. Great ships at Gibraltar fired the salute ; at Malta trumpeters sounded the Last Post ; in Jamaica the members of the Legislature went from church to their Senate House to hold a special meeting of sorrow and loyalty. In remote islands scattered over the oceans of the world grief for the King showed itself in like manner.

Wherever British people dwell in foreign lands, they too met together in their own churches, and found that their hosts were eager to be with them. Cardinals and princes of the Papal Court attended the solemn service of intercession for stricken England, and King Victor Emmanuel, with Signor Mussolini, who had been among the first to condole with the British Royal Family, joined in the service at the Anglican church in Rome. King Alfonso was also present ; in his former capital four consecutive and identical services were held at the English church, so many were the mourners. At Washington the heads of the American Government, with the wife of the President, attended a thronged cathedral. The Bishop of New York spoke eloquently of " a most noble example of a constitutional ruler." In Geneva a congregation representative of many nations paid honour to one of the greatest friends of peace. Throughout France there was spontaneous grief for the end of a long companionship, proven under stress of war. In Germany former enemies, famous soldiers among them, were led by Herr Hitler himself in tribute to the King's memory, and the Führer spoke words of personal sympathy to the British Ambassador. The flag of the Reich yielded place to the Union Jack in every ship of the German Navy. Princes of the House of Hohenzollern, with King Ferdinand, late of Bulgaria, accompanied the mourners. So the messages came pouring in telling of commemorations bewilderingly various in detail, all identical in sentiment. The widowed Queen-Mother of Belgium made her first official reappearance in public to mourn for her dead husband's friend. From Lisbon and Cairo, from Montevideo and Jerusalem, from Vienna, from Tunis, from Constantinople, from Warsaw, Budapest, and Prague came the same story. Everywhere the people and their rulers, each according to their own national customs, placed themselves in spirit beside the mourning multitudes in distant London. Even in the remote lands of China and Japan the guns sounded and the flags flew at half-mast.

These things pass, but they are not lost nor forgotten. They show that the things that unite men and nations, though less often visible, are more fundamental and more universal than the things that divide. A life nobly lived according to the code of one people is noble also by the standards of peoples far away, though formal creeds may differ and material interests clash. In our moments of loss we all cease in one another's eyes to be strangers, political opponents, economic competitors, heretics, or infidels, and are seen as fellow-men. Something of that understanding of reality must remain when the pang of which it was

The arrival of the gun-carriage at Paddington Station.

The funeral train on the way from Paddington to Windsor.

born has been softened by the hand of time. Meanwhile the British people are grateful for the sympathy of all the world, and both the sympathy and the gratitude are stones to be built into the arch of peace.

BY THE PRIME MINISTER

The Prime Minister broadcast the following message to the nation on January 21 :

" After he had served his own generation by the will of God he fell on sleep and was laid unto his fathers."

Those words kept recurring to me in the watches of last night, for if there was one thing that our King had done it was to serve his own generation by the will of God, and because of that the news of the death of His Majesty, when it came, has been heard everywhere with a personal grief, not only in this country, but through the vast Empire over which he bore rule, and, I believe, far beyond its borders.

To famous men all the earth is a sepulchre. It is less than a month ago that the voice now silent was heard around the world, a King addressing his subjects, a father seated with his family speaking to his people, members of his wider family, words of wisdom, courage, and deep human sympathy. And it is as members of a family that we are mourning him to-day. There must be millions who feel as I do that a wise and loving friend and counsellor has been taken from us, and for long the world will seem a poorer and a colder place without him, and the tones of that well-known voice are echoing in our ears to-day as our thoughts turn to the widowed Queen and to the bereaved family.

And I do want to say a word to you about Queen Mary, for I know that every heart in the Empire is sore for her this night. It often seems to me that in a married life so perfect, so happy as theirs was, there has to come that inevitable day when one is taken and the other is left, and one of the two has to continue the pilgrimage to the end alone. There are millions of hands which, if they could reach the Queen, would be stretched out to her and tears of sympathy be shed with her, and it must be some comfort to her, though we cannot tell her that, to know of that feeling, and she must know it from the events of that wonderful Jubilee summer but may not this be a comfort to her as it has been a comfort to others, that, after all, the one who is left is really carrying the cross for the one who has gone before ?

If she were not suffering to-day, he would be, and she is bearing what might have been his sorrow for him ; and I cannot help feeling that with a King, knowing how lonely the high places of the world are, and knowing that he has no one but his wife with whom he might have really intimate converse—I tremble to think what it might have been for him had he been alone in his awful task with no voice by him to cheer, to comfort, and to encourage. We are thankful indeed to feel that even in her sorrow Queen Mary is spared to the people who love her, and I am sure that we all of us, all our people, will show her in whatever way they can how close she is to their hearts and how they will treasure her not only for the King's sake but for her own.

And as to the King, what can I say in a few minutes, and within twenty-four hours of this shattering blow ? I think I may dwell for these few minutes on the King as I have known him during this last year, and try to picture him as one who has borne the responsibilities of his position during perhaps the most difficult quarter of a century in which a monarch has ever sat on our Throne. There was no respite for him during those twenty-five years. The whole world has been in a state of commotion, and there never seemed to come to him any period when he could look ahead for two or three years and feel that all would be peace and quiet and nothing in the world to cause him or his people trouble. The world has been what a great man of the sixteenth century called it, " a raving world," and he played his part in it gallantly to the end, and I do feel most thankful that after that illness of his six years ago he was spared to see that Jubilee year.

He and his Ministers and his doctors and, I think, all who knew much about these things felt some apprehension as to the strain he might have to undergo in attending the various ceremonies and functions that belonged to that time. But all our fears were belied, for there seemed to be given to him a special strength to go through those weeks. And I rejoice that he, modest as ever, diffident as to his own powers, often wondering what his people thought of what he had done and tried to do for them—I often think that it was a most wonderful experience for him to see, to have brought home to him, that all he had done had sunk deep into their hearts. The occasion of that Jubilee was the occasion that they all embraced to throw off that shyness so characteristic of us and show him openly and without shame that they were proud of him as their King, that they loved him as a man.

The effect on him, I think, was great. He never referred to it without emotion. He was touched profoundly. He accepted that tribute with a thankful humility. I am indeed thankful that he lived to see it and that during the last months he knew what he meant to his people. But we knew that there was no strength to spare. To go through that last illness had taken from him every reserve of strength that he had. We knew that it must go hard with him if any illness should attack him, even were it a slight one, and I myself noticed in the months that followed the Jubilee— and I have never known him so gentle, so calm—an increase even of his customary consideration, his customary kindliness, and I had a feeling, which I expressed to my friends, through all the autumn that he was ready for the long journey that he was so soon to take.

He was tired at times, and I used to contrast his lot with the lot of the politicians, for we can and do have our old age, if we live, to ourselves. But the King's burden is never lifted. It goes on all through the year, and it goes on with age, and the only release from it is death. And then, again, you will remember the death of his sister. Many who are listening to me to-night may be elderly brothers and sisters, perhaps between 60 and 70 years of age. You know what a link that is, the common memories of childhood, and there are few losses as men and women get older, few losses that strike so deep as those of contemporary relations with their share of common memories. And it was no ordinary bond, no formal bond, that united the King and his sister. They were devoted to each other, and His Majesty, if he had not seen her, would talk to her on the telephone every night and tell her what he had been doing to cheer her and make her life less lonely. I think that he felt the severance of that old tie very keenly.

I saw him for the last time when we parted for the Christmas holidays. It is the only time in the year that I am able to go to my own home, and he was going to his at Sandringham, and we were rejoicing together, for we both loved the same kind of holiday, and we were going to spend it with our own children and with our grandchildren at our own home in the country. It was but a few days after that when the first intimation reached us that all was not well. At the end of last week and during the week-end I was in constant touch with Sandringham, and it was only yesterday morning the King's Secretary rang me up to tell me that he had seen a change, and that he feared that the end could not be long delayed.

There is one thing I think I can tell you without any impropriety, for though much, and most indeed, of what passes near the end is sacred, and we none of us have the desire or right to inquire into what happened at those times, yet I think I may tell you this. The King was having brief intervals of consciousness, and each time he became conscious it was some kind inquiry or kind observation of someone, some words of gratitude for kindness shown. But he did say to his secretary when he sent for him : " How is the Empire ? " An unusual phrase in that form, and the secretary said : " All is well, sir, with the Empire," and the King gave him a smile and relapsed once more into unconsciousness.

It was simply this, that during all that time subconsciously and just coming to the surface at odd moments was that same love for his people, care for their well-being here and throughout the world, for that family to whom he spoke last Christmas, and the thought of them was with him to the end. King George, it is true, inherited his position on the Throne, but he won his own way to the hearts of his people. Behind the pomp and the pageantry incidental to his great position he laboured night and day in that high station to which God had called him. The doing of his duty to the utmost of his ability was the guiding principle of his life.

Great power which corrupts weak natures ennobled our King's character and made him subdue passion and will and energy to his duty to his country. He brought the dispositions that are lovely in private life into the service and conduct of the Common-wealth, and not only in virtue of his office but in virtue of his person was he the first gentleman in the land. As the knowledge of the King's complete dedication to duty grew and spread as his reign proceeded, so did the respect of his people turn into reverence, and reverence into love. It is literally true that he won their hearts, and during the Jubilee they made that manifest to him.

This is the truth we must bear in mind as we think of the son who succeeds to the Throne and upon whom has now fallen one of the heaviest burdens that can rest upon the shoulders of fallible and mortal man. We can best honour the noble memory of King George by gathering round and sustaining the young King whom for so long we have delighted to know as the Prince of Wales. All eyes are upon him as he advances to his father's place, and, while he is no stranger to public duty, he is now summoned to face responsibilities more onerous, more exacting, more continuous than any he has hitherto been asked to discharge.

He comes to them in the prime of his powers, and already known throughout the length and breadth of his Empire. His great gifts of mind and heart he is now called upon to consecrate to his people. He inherits an example of kingly conduct, of virtue, of wisdom, and of endurance. King George's reign was marked by far-reaching constitutional and Parliamentary changes without precedent in our long history. He earned the loyalty and respect of all parties in the State, new and old. He hands down in turn to his son the Throne he himself received from his father, and he hands it down with its foundations strengthened, its moral authority, its honour, and its dignity enhanced. It is an incomparable and awe-inspiring inheritance.

The young King knows the confidence we all repose in him. He knows that he commands not only the allegiance, he knows that the understanding, the affection, and the prayers of the countless multitudes of his subjects are with him at this hour. May God guide him aright and God Save the King.

BY THE ARCHBISHOP OF CANTERBURY

Memorial services for King George were held all over the country on the day of the funeral. Cathedrals and churches were filled with citizens, led in their mourning by civic and other public representatives, and in many places overflow services were held. Services were relayed to waiting crowds outside. Public squares and market places where events of national significance are celebrated often proved inadequate for the large crowds which gathered to observe the Two Minutes Silence. On the Sunday before the funeral, that is, January 26, ordinary Church services were made the occasion of tributes to King George's memory. The following is the substance of the Archbishop of Canterbury's sermon in Westminster Abbey on that day :

Taking his text from Daniel x. 19, " O man greatly beloved, peace be unto thee," Dr. Lang said that these were words which came most naturally and fitly into their hearts as they thought of the King whose body lay within a stone's throw of the Abbey. Let them be, as it were, a message which, as sorrowing yet thankful subjects, they sent to him now.

It is perhaps not easy [he continued] for us under the pressure of a great immediate sorrow to foresee what place the verdict of history will give to King George V in the long line of British Kings. Yet I venture to predict that that verdict will confirm the simple, spontaneous judgment expressed last week by a workman at my Lambeth home : " We never had a better."

Assuredly there have been Kings and Queens more powerful, more forcible, more romantic in the circumstances of their lives, and who have exercised a more commanding influence on the public affairs of their time. Yet here, in the region of public influence, the future historian must give a high place to King George. For he will see more clearly than we can that his reign was marked by changes, in the extension of the franchise, and in the Constitution of the Realm and the Empire, more far-reaching than in almost any previous reign ; and that through all these changes the position of the Monarchy was not only maintained but strengthened. He will recognize that this could not have been possible unless the King himself had been a man of most marked tact and self-control and resolute loyalty to the principles of Constitutional government. The historian will be the more impressed because the memorials of King George which he will possess will show him to have been a man of strong personal opinions, wont to express them to his friends in singularly forcible terms. The historian will record that, while either personal weakness or self-assertion would have endangered the Monarchy, the mingled strength and self-restraint of King George made it stronger than ever before.

In the second place our historian will most certainly record that these twenty-five years, including as they did the Great War and all the economic disorders which followed it, put the spirit of the British people to a severer test than at any other time in their history. When he asks how it was that the people kept so united, so resolute, his inquiry will bring him to the influence of the King, who in the midst of all anxieties stood himself so steadfast and confident and courageous that he became the symbol and centre of the nation's unity and strength. Yes, even when he measures by these tests of beneficent public influence will not the historian be bound to ask, " After all, has Britain ever had a better King ? "

But to us, his contemporaries, his own subjects, the title of King George to a place among the best of British Kings rests upon a surer, deeper basis. It is that he was a man greatly beloved. Of that fact there can be no doubt. The celebrations of the Silver Jubilee year and the solemnities of this last week are over-whelming evidence. Make all allowances for the new powers of publicity, with their undoubted effect in creating mass emotion ; is there record in our history of any such demonstration, so spontaneous, so universal, of a great stirring of the common heart ?

I remember well the funeral of Queen Victoria, as I was privileged to take a part, small, but to me most moving. It was beyond all words impressive—the little yacht bearing the Queen's body passing through the lines of great battleships as they thundered their last salute, and coming to anchor as the winter sun set in a blaze of crimson gold ; the vast crowds lining the shores ; next day the procession moving through the streets of London in a silence that could be felt. It was reverence for the great Queen and a sense almost of awe at the passing of a great epoch that moved the multitude.

I remember also the funeral of King Edward VII, and the genuine sorrow at the vanishing from our sight of a King so gracious, so full of charm, vitality, and rich humanity. But I cannot remember in either case just that same all-pervading sense of personal bereavement springing from a sense of personal affection.

The long lines of people who have been passing the body of King George as it lies in the silent storied spaces of Westminster Hall must have felt, " Here lies a man greatly beloved." We never had a better King, because never a King was more loved by his people.

Of that fact there can be no doubt ; but how is it to be explained ? The question is more easily asked than answered.

King George himself, speaking to me about all those overwhelming evidences of loyalty which the Silver Jubilee called forth, used some words so characteristic of his honesty and humility that I cannot refrain from repeating them even in these surroundings. I seem to hear him say them now. " I am sure I cannot understand it, for, after all, I am only a very ordinary sort of fellow." There was a truth in those simple words which he himself could not discern, for the secret of the power of his personality over his people was, I think, as I have said elsewhere, that they came to see in him just the sort of man each of them instinctively would wish to be—simple, sincere, frank, a lover of home and of healthy sport, loyal to his friends, keeping a high standard of personal life and public duty, steadfast in service, and mindful of his God. Such a man his people understood. They saw in him the simple sterling virtues which each of them knew to be right for himself. This was the personality which more and more fully as the years passed communicated itself to the people.

In the later time of his life he was enabled by the marvellous invention of the wireless to come into direct touch with them all throughout every part of his far-reaching Empire. When they heard his own voice and the simple, strong, sincere words he spoke, they felt more than ever he was in the best sense one of themselves, that they belonged to each other, bound by ties of mutual understanding and trust, and that he was a true father of them all.

Beneath this personality, which thus gradually and surely became so greatly beloved, was a foundation which in this place, this central shrine of our national Christianity, must be specially remembered. It was his religion. There are only two words needed to describe King George's religion. It was simple. It was real. Simple certainly. There were great and rich regions of religion to which he was a comparative stranger ; ecclesiastical, emotional, sacramental, mystical. His religion was based on an all-abiding sense of his responsibility and his duty to God. If we use the old words, the fear of God, in their true Bible sense, as a reverent remembrance of God's reality and claim, King George was a God-fearing man. A simple religion, but very real. It was expressed in certain habits of life of which he said little, but which he resolutely kept : his daily prayers, his daily reading of the Bible—I doubt whether any layman had a more accurate, if not always fully instructed, knowledge of the Bible ; Sunday

The funeral procession passing through Lower Ward at Windsor Castle.

after Sunday, wherever he might be, his presence at the public worship of God.

I cannot but remember at this moment that twenty-four years ago, at his Coronation, speaking from this place, I tried in a few words to describe the true sovereignty of service. He lived to wield that sovereignty most fully. I am sure that it was in his deep sense of responsibility to God that he found the motive and the support for his sense of responsibility to the nation and for his unwearying service. To the very end he was unswerving in his devotion to duty. It may be that some of you have read the description I ventured to give to the House of Lords last Thursday of his very last public act, a few hours before his death—that last most pathetic but most gallant rally to the old claim of duty. Deep down in that inner region where dwell the ultimate motives of life his duty to God stood strong. However limited a religion so simple may seem to be, it met the great requirements of all religion, to do justly, to love mercy, and to walk humbly with God.

So he has passed from us—this man greatly beloved. God bless him and keep him. But are we content to let him pass into the silence leaving nothing but a memory behind? Must not our love and loyalty bid us not only keep his memory within us but also keep his example before us? Through that example " he, being dead, yet speaketh," and the voice which had become so familiar to us can still be heard. Mindful of that example, let me, as I close, ask two things of you, his people, while your hearts are stilled and solemnized by sorrow.

The first is this : recover simplicity of life. It is a phrase often used to advocate all sorts of artificial contrivances, but the true simplification of life must come from within, from the region of the soul. Truly it is needed. For a hundred reasons our modern life is becoming increasingly complicated, tangled, confused. We have need to recover those old, strong, sterling virtues to which our nation and every nation has given homage in the homage that was given to King George. In the midst of the whirl of amusements keep a steadying rule of duty. In the midst of all temptations to selfishness, to get for ourselves all that life can bring us, keep a place for some disinterested service to others, especially to those to whom life seems to bring so little ; let service come before self. While marriage is being treated with so much recklessness and frivolity, remember the home life of King George, and keep your own homes pure and stable. When a hundred voices in fiction, in the Press, and in talk are muddling and confusing conscience, set before yourselves some fixed standard of personal integrity and honour below which you will scorn to fall. Prove in your own lives what King George proved in his : that simplicity is strength.

And let none think that this discipline will deprive life of its true pleasures. It will but clear away the weeds. With all his self-discipline King George himself loved life and sport and laughter. It is always to the true of heart that there springs up joyful gladness. Fundamental truth of heart—that is our need.

The second thing I would ask of you for his sake is—recover remembrance of God. In the ever-increasing speed of mere physical movement, " faster and faster " seems to be becoming almost a motto of existence. The haste and hurry and distraction of life infect the soul. In the mere jostle of sensations and of opinions we have no time to stop and think, and God is crowded out. Yet it is sternly true that, without some inner hold on God neither man nor nation can be stable and strong. Let us take heed to the warning uttered in the days of our prosperity by that poet and prophet whose ashes have just been buried beneath the floor of this Abbey Church :

> Lord God of Hosts, be with us yet
> Lest we forget—lest we forget.

Let the steadfast, God-fearing King speak to us from the world of eternal truth into which he has passed. " O my people, remember, remember the Lord God of your Fathers." For us still the struggle, wherein his example may quiet us, steady us, and keep us true ; for him the eternal rest. As on Tuesday morning I looked for the last time upon the face of my King, my friend, and wondered at the light of beautiful serenity which lay upon it, it seemed to me as if a greeting had already come to him from beyond the veil : " O man greatly beloved, peace be to thee."

THE BROADCAST SERVICE

The service to the memory of King George V which was broadcast was deeply impressive to the relatively few who were privileged to hear it, as it were, behind the microphone at Broadcasting House. The concert hall where it was held gave a sense of detachment, and the immediate audience, which included the Governors of the B.B.C., might have been inclined, but for the fittings and apparatus, to forget the vast unseen audience without.

The audience at Broadcasting House stood at only two parts of the service—first, when the orchestra played the Dead March in *Saul*, and at the end, when the National Anthem was sung. The Archbishop of Canterbury, who delivered a moving tribute to the late King, sat before a microphone which was placed on a small purple-covered table. On the large platform behind were grouped the orchestra and the chorus.

The service, the music of which was arranged by Sir Walford Davies, Master of the King's Musick, began with the hymn, " O love that wilt not let me go." Dr. S. M. Berry, Moderator of the Federal Council of Evangelical Churches, read the lesson, taken from Revelation, beginning with the words, " And I saw a new heaven and a new earth," and special prayers were said by the Rev. Professor Daniel Lamont, Moderator-designate of the Church of Scotland.

In the course of his address the Archbishop of Canterbury said :

It is difficult for me to speak, because to me personally the passing of King George means the loss of a personal friendship with which he had honoured me for nearly forty years, and because few days have passed since I stood at his side and commended his soul to God as he passed from our sight. Yet perhaps this very difficulty may give to you who are listening to me the assurance that such words as I am able to speak come from the depths of my heart.

I have been asked to speak about King George himself, his own personality. I venture to say that the impression made by that personality upon the whole Realm and Empire is one of the most striking facts in the long history of this nation. The experience of this last memorable week—the words spoken in Parliament, the tributes received from every part of the Empire and of the world, the demeanour of the crowds who have watched the body passing through the streets of London, the solemnity of the tense silence when it was received in Westminster Hall by the Parliament of the Realm, the sense which could be felt of a great fellowship of sorrow uniting all classes—all this has made it plain that somehow or other this simple and truly humble man had drawn his people everywhere to himself by the ties of a most real personal attachment.

From beginning to end King George had to face a constant series of crises, each of them most anxious, one of them the most exacting ordeal through which the British nation had ever passed. Once, as I was walking with him in his Highland hills, he said to me, somewhat sadly, that he seemed to be destined again and again to encounter national difficulties, each one of them more searching than any which had occurred in the more than sixty years of the reign of Queen Victoria, and he asked " Will there never be an end of them ? " Think of all that lay behind such words as these, marking successive periods of his reign—Ireland, the Parliament Act, the Great War, the general strike, the economic crisis five years ago.

King George was not endowed with any conspicuous gifts of body or mind. True, he had a most accurate memory, a sound judgment which, dismissing irrelevant matters, went to the core of complicated questions, and an ever-growing experience. But he himself would always lament that he came to the Throne with no fuller education than that which was given to a sailor voyaging on the sea—an education admirable in itself, but scarcely wide enough as an introduction to public affairs. Moreover, he never possessed the arts, and certainly never practised the devices, by which popularity is often secured. Yet gradually and surely, in spite of all, his personality came through.

As crisis after crisis came and passed, his people became conscious of the quiet courage, the confident trust, the unswerving devotion to duty with which he met them. They felt that at the centre of the national life there was a man strong, confident, steadfast, and that in their King there was one who both represented and strengthened the unity and stability of the Empire. He had enhanced the prestige and value of the Throne. But it was through the personal affection which he had drawn from the hearts of his people that he gave " a new significance to the name of King."

The knowledge of this growing personal feeling towards himself supported and strengthened him in all anxieties. You may remember the words which he used in his message on the Christmas Day before the Silver Jubilee year : " If I may be regarded as in some true sense the head of this great and widespread family, sharing its life and sustained by its affection, this will be a full reward for the long and sometimes anxious labours of my reign." In the celebrations of that memorable year the reward was overwhelmingly given to him. They gave him overwhelming evidence not only of the loyalty but of the love he had inspired. I think the strength of it surprised him. What pleased him especially was the knowledge that it was in the heart of common folk that this personal affection lay.

He himself told us how deeply touched and stirred he was in his broadcast message on May 6. He said : " I can only say to you, my very dear people, that the Queen and I thank you from the depths of our hearts for all the loyalty and—may I say ?—the love with which this day and always you have surrounded us. I dedicate myself anew to your service for the years that may still be given to me." No further years were to be given. But we may be most thankful that in his last year he knew how truly he had enthroned himself in the common heart. The universal sorrow now has been offered not so much to a King as to a friend and father of his people.

His unswerving devotion to duty upheld him to the end. Twelve hours before his death, sitting very thin and frail on his chair, he held a meeting of his Privy Council. To the Order constituting a Council of State he gave in his old, clear voice the familiar " Approved." He was asked whether he wished to sign the Order with his own hand. " Yes," he said, " I have always signed myself." But his hands could not grasp the pen. For several minutes they moved to and fro across the paper, and then, with a most moving act of his old courtesy, he turned to his

Council and said, " I am very sorry to keep you waiting so long," and added, after a pause, " You see, I cannot concentrate." For some minutes still the hands renewed their attempts, most gallant and most pathetic, to sign. At last he was content to make a mark, and then, with his old kindly, kingly smile, he bade his Council farewell. It was a scene which we who witnessed it can never forget. It showed that in his last conscious hour he was true to his lifelong fidelity to the claim of duty.

Again, I recall his loyalty to his friends—not least to his old shipmates. Some of us will always remember that one of the favourite endings of his personal letters was "Your old friend." It is these old friends who will sorrow most that never again will they see his kindly smile or hear his hearty laughter and his vivid and emphatic talk.

When last Tuesday morning I saw this little head resting in peace upon the pillow I could not but reflect that all the dignities which surround a King had been laid aside and that there were left only the two ultimate realities—the man himself and God. . . . Let the voice of this steadfast, God-fearing King speak to us now. " O my people, remember, remember the Lord God of your fathers." He himself is now passing through the Valley of the Shadow of Death. It is enough to know that he need fear no evil, for God is with him. It seemed to me as I looked for the last time upon his face that the beautiful serenity and peace which lay upon it was itself a sign that he had entered into the rest that remains for the people of God.

Queen Mary has her own place in our thoughts and prayers. No words are needed to remind you of the wonderful comradeship she gave King George for more than forty years, a comradeship of unfailing love and counsel and strength. During these last anxious days she has shown a truly noble fortitude, as I can testify. She has given to all who surrounded her the example and support of unbroken calmness and strength. The pressure of deep emotion was always ready to break through, but it was held in wonderful self-control. The whole people offer to her a deep and understanding sympathy. We pray God that His Spirit may uphold and strengthen her, and that for many years to come she may be with us and enjoy in ever fuller measure the possession of the hearts of her people.

The procession approaching St. George's Chapel, Windsor.

The naval gun's crew and the gun-carriage at St. George's Chapel, Windsor.

What shall we say of our new King—" the Prince " whose name has become a household word throughout the Nation and Empire ? We all know how eager he has ever proved to be in seeing with his own eyes the real life of the people in all parts of the Empire, in caring for the unemployed, and in giving the youth of the country a better chance of a full life. No other Monarch, it may be said, has ever come to the Throne knowing so well and known so intimately by all classes of his subjects. The new King has a personality of his own, in many ways different from that of his beloved father, and it is through his own personality that he must make his contribution to the history of the British Monarchy. We pray that his gifts may be consecrated to the service of his people and of God, and that his character may be so deepened and strengthened that he may rise nobly to the height of his new and great responsibility.

The King is dead. God receive him. Long live the King. God bless, and guide, and strengthen him !

THE HOUSE OF LORDS

The following speeches were made in the House of Lords on the moving of addresses to King Edward VIII and to Queen Mary :

LORD HALIFAX.—We meet here this afternoon, as it were, to say farewell in Parliament to one whom we can ill afford to lose. For more than five and twenty years King George was Sovereign and truly father of all who owed allegiance to him, and we can as yet scarcely measure the full significance of the place he had come to hold among us.

These islands have known Kings from the beginnings of their history, but I doubt whether throughout the centuries there has been any whose lot was cast in times at home and abroad of such continuing anxiety. Always mindful of the obligation laid upon him to be the guardian of his country's rights and liberties and faithful to the spirit of the Constitution of which he was the sworn upholder, King George constantly pointed the path of moderation when the fires of party strife blazed dangerously.

In the hard test of war we recall how much of the will to endurance was inspired by his leadership and example, as in more recent years we acknowledged how greatly it was due to his encouragement that the nation never lost confidence in itself to win through the darkest days of industrial depression. Strong in his own faith, he was able to inspire others with a courage which matched his own ; and so events that brought adversity to other Monarchs served only here to strengthen the foundations of the Throne and to increase the stature of the King.

But his death has been more than the passing of a great King. In every sense of the word he and those he ruled belonged to one another, for the years had brought a singular quality of understanding from which grew the most complete confidence between them. Throughout his reign his subjects had seen in what fashion he devoted himself to the multifarious duties of his high station, and came more and more to realize what it meant to them and to all they cared for most that such an example should be set before them.

Therefore to-day there is no home under the British flag that does not miss his presence and feel a sense of personal loss. First gentleman in the land, he taught us that only he who serves can rightly claim that title ; it was through service he became the familiar friend and counsellor of all his people. They learnt by countless acts of simple kindness that no interest, sorrow, or joy of theirs was outside his thought, or too humble for his sympathy, and they were not slow to repay so great a debt by spontaneous and deep affection. Something of this they had an opportunity of showing last year, when all classes of the King's subjects in all parts of his Dominions seized the occasion to manifest the full measure and strength of what they felt towards him. It was characteristic of the King's natural humility that this exhibition of the Empire's love should have been to him at all surprising.

The words he spoke only last Christmas, a short month ago, from Sandringham, showed that at last he realized what we then, by the only means open to us all, had meant to say to him, and with what feeling he had received our message.

The King dies, but the King's place is filled, for the Crown is the keystone of our Imperial fellowship, and that which is the hallowed object of the highest loyalty of the whole British Commonwealth, the very symbol of its unity, can never die. King Edward comes to the Throne no stranger here or in the wider confines of his Empire. We have long known how powerful is the appeal made to his sympathies by everything that affects the lot of the least fortunate of his fellow-men. As did his father he brings to his new responsibilities a personal knowledge gained by direct contacts that is of inestimable worth. While to-day we sympathize with the King in the loss of a beloved father, and proffer to him our respectful loyalty on the occasion of his Accession, most earnestly do we pray that his reign may be long in years and abundantly blessed in the love and prosperity of all his subjects.

At this time there is one thought uppermost in all our minds, which finds expression in the address that I have the honour to move to Her Majesty Queen Mary. We must naturally be reluctant to intrude upon the privacy of the great sorrow felt by those nearest to the late King, and we all know how limited is the capacity of mere human sympathy to redeem the sadness of it. Yet none the less we would wish to convey to Her Majesty how deeply we have revered that Royal partnership, perfect in the intimacy of home as in the full light of public life, which death has so suddenly dissolved.

There will have been none of your lordships present in Westminster Hall just now who had not in mind the last time King George came to his Palace of Westminster and addressed his Parliament in that historic hall of William Rufus. And those of us who then attended on His Majesty will not soon forget that part of his speech wherein he paid tribute to the help of her who had been Queen and wife for so many years, and by that acknowledgment gave the world a glimpse of what that help had been. We may humbly ask Almighty God to help and comfort her, and to give healing power to the tide of sympathy and gratitude that flows to her from the hearts of all her people.

LORD SNELL.—Upon me falls the privilege and the duty of supporting the motion which with a rare dignity has been proposed by the noble viscount Lord Halifax. I shall try to complete my task with an appropriate brevity, but with a sympathy which is not less profound than that expressed by the Leader of the House.

We are united in the desire to receive and pass this motion, and any lengthy commendation of it would in consequence be inopportune and superfluous. It is none the less advisable, if only to indicate the universal sympathy which is felt for Queen Mary and the members of the Royal House in the great loss they have sustained in the death of the beloved Head of their family, that as representing the Opposition Party in your lordships' House I should speak briefly in support of it. The death of King George, the faithful and long-trusted Head of the State, is for many of us a personal as well as a great public loss. But my individual feelings at the end of a long and nobly completed life are not restricted to the grief which comes with the knowledge that henceforth a dear and guiding personality will not be seen among us.

I have in addition to this natural human sorrow a sense of quiet inner rejoicing for the rare quality of the life that was—a feeling of glad pride in the duty so long continued and so loyally and courageously performed, and satisfaction that in him great ends were so nobly served. King George in his proper person set before us an inspiring example of dignified simplicity and of fidelity to the anxious and exacting responsibilities of his great position. Associated as I am, and as we all are, with our fellow-countrymen in their sorrow, I have nevertheless a personal feeling of joyful gratitude for the triumph in him of the human spirit and for all that that implied for us.

It is appropriate for me to say a few words from the standpoint of the Labour Party, which I specially represent. We honoured the King as the responsible Head of the State, and we were always meticulously careful not to cause him embarrassment either by associating his name with our own proposals or by connecting him with those of other parties. We regarded him as the symbol of the nation's unity and character and thought of him as being the impartial friend and chief servant of his people, separate from, and living above, the uneasy storms and perplexing divisions of the political arena. On that high plane we were content to leave him, expecting from him and receiving from him the impartial consideration that belonged to his detached position and giving to him in return a full, spontaneous, and never-varying loyalty.

It is a sound and accepted principle of our British life that the Head of the State should be no respecter of parties, that he should be detached from, and unaffected by, the passion of dividing enthusiasms which form a necessary and desirable part of our daily political experience. King George exactly fitted this type and its requirements, and he received from his people a spontaneous affection and trust. It was the fate, and perhaps also the good fortune, of the King to rule over the State at a most interesting and crucial period in the world's history. It was a time of rapidly expanding vision, of many acute crises, and of great change. During his reign the principles on which our State is founded were subjected to frequent and severe strains. They bore the burden without disaster. Our English ways were justified and even strengthened by our own experiences. King George was a living symbol of our free spirit and free institutions. He had the united support of his subjects, in whose affection and trust he had great happiness, and was assured of a personal security such as no armed protection could have given.

I could not without presumption speak of the late King as a man, for I did not know him as he was known to most of your lordships. But it is permissible, I hope, for me to say that on the few occasions when I had the privilege of meeting him I was received by him with the unaffected, spontaneous, and genial courtesy of a great gentleman. My lords, there is nothing further that I need say, but on behalf of my noble friends, and also on behalf of those whom they and I represent outside these walls, I very regretfully and sincerely commend this motion to your approval.

I beg, finally, specially to associate myself and my noble friends with that part of the motion which congratulates His Majesty King Edward VIII on his accession to the Throne. His Majesty will, I hope, not resent my saying that from the day of his birth the older among his subjects have watched with keen interest and ever-increasing satisfaction his development, his industry, his wide sympathies, and, above all, his constant and careful preparation for the great task that he now has to face. Perhaps more closely than any previous Monarch, he knows the needs of the poorer sections of his people. He has seen them on the tragic field of battle, in the mills and mines and fields of this country. He has seen the housing conditions under which many of them live, and he has seen something of their sufferings when faced with the grim realities of unemployment.

It may well be that at this hour His Majesty distrusts the extent of his own powers as he looks upon the task that faces him, the demands upon his strength that will be made. May he be helped by the assurance that we this day convey to him, that behind him now and in the future are the understanding sympathy and trust of his people, whose satisfaction in his proved qualities may well be greater at this time than his own faith in himself. I beg to support the motion.

LORD MOTTISTONE.—In the absence of Lord Crewe through illness I have been asked to support the two motions before your lordships, which have been moved and supported already, on behalf of all those who sit in this part of the House. Like Lord Crewe, I was in the Liberal Cabinet before the War, and there learned, as has been said by Lord Snell, His Majesty's complete impartiality and desire to help every party in the State. I learned, too, as a Minister, as all Ministers have done, his intense devotion to duty. Nothing would ever prevent His Majesty from fulfilling every duty, large or small ; answering every question and every letter on the day it was received. It was marvellous how he got through the work.

But more than that. As your lordships will well remember, dark shadows spread across our land before the War. I think all those who had to do with those dark days will agree—and I am sure that history will record—that while preserving strictly every Constitutional duty and principle, His late Majesty's intervention, initiative, and wise counsel saved this land from great perils in a way which no other man could have saved it.

And so it was that we entered upon the War a united people, a united nation, and all of us, like so many of your lordships, who spent those four years on the Western front, cannot forget the visits of our late Sovereign, the short addresses which he gave to the troops. You will remember, my lords who were there, that there was not one of us whom he addressed—and on his many visits to the front line, regardless of all risks or discomforts, he addressed altogether hundreds of thousands of his troops—who was not heartened and found the task before us was less hard. Indeed, we owe him a deep debt for that.

The coffin being carried into St. George's Chapel, Windsor.

Then, as happened to so many of us, when we were in hospital after some time in the front line, when wounds befel us, the Queen would come and visit us in hospital. I am sure I speak for tens of thousands of soldiers whom her Majesty the Queen visited in hospital in saying that they owe more to her than they can ever repay. To each one she spoke as though she cared for him deeply for himself—as indeed she did. Without doubt, as many of those who had charge of the front-line hospitals have told us, Her Majesty actually saved the lives of hundreds of fighting men, whose failing spirits were revived by this gracious lady's kindly words. We do not forget it, and all of us without exception, and especially those to whom I have referred, join in profound sympathy with Her Majesty in the great loss that has befallen her.

All the time his present Majesty was sharing to the full the dangers of the front line, so that in our darkest hour we could truly say that we owed more than can ever be said in words to the late King, to the Queen, and to his present Majesty for their help and example in those dark days of peril and war. When the War came to an end it so happened that I was brought into close contact with His late Majesty and got to know him well. It was impossible to converse with him, as I did year after year, and not to realize that you could say of His late Majesty, as you can hardly say of anyone else whom I have met, that he was so unselfish a man that he cared more for each one of his subjects than he cared for himself.

He loved the sea with a passionate love. The lifeboats were his constant care and interest ; for forty-six years he was closely identified with them. He cared deeply, of course, for the Royal Navy and the Mercantile Marine, and for his yacht Britannia. Those who saw him at the wheel of his yacht, with the spray dashing across his face or the yacht he loved so well forging forward in a stiff breeze, realized to the full how greatly the King could enjoy all healthy sports.

He loved all good things, he hated all that was mean and unfair. I suppose it is not untrue to say that while this Realm and this Empire has lost a great Sovereign, every man, woman, and child has lost in His late Majesty a real, true, devoted, unselfish friend.

The ARCHBISHOP OF CANTERBURY.—It is perhaps natural that on this memorable occasion I should say some words as representing the lords spiritual in your lordships' House, but if I may say

L

so it is perhaps more natural that they should be spoken by one whom His late Majesty honoured with a friendship of more than forty years and who had the privilege of standing by his side as his spirit was passing to the unseen world.

It may be that history will not speak of his reign as a happy reign, for, indeed, it was marked throughout by great crises, each one of them most formidable and one of them the most bitter ordeal through which this country had ever had to pass. But assuredly it was happy because of the constancy and courage with which through these difficulties he was able to inspire his people and because of the love and loyalty which they showed to him.

I doubt very much whether anyone in our long history has ever enjoyed an affection so intimate and personal. It was the knowledge of this, as I well know, that inspired and cheered him during all these anxieties. Your lordships may remember the words which he used on the Christmas Day before his Silver Jubilee year. They are worth reminding your lordships of. He said : " If I may be regarded as in some true sense the head of this great and widespread family, sharing its life and sustained by its affection, this will be a full reward for the long and sometimes anxious labours of my reign."

In the celebrations of that memorable year he received that reward in full measure, pressed down and running over. I know how deeply moved and stirred was his heart. The tribute was the more remarkable because he was the last man to claim that he had received conspicuous gifts either of body or of mind, the last man who would ever have attempted to court popularity, and he was content to be at all times and to all persons just himself.

But it was that natural self of his that won so remarkably the respect and affection of his people. By one of those instincts which belong to a free people they discerned in their King just the sort of man that each one of them would wish to be—simple, sincere, straightforward in speech and act, loyal to home and friend, a lover of sport, yet unflinching in his devotion to duty, and, as the basis of all great character, mindful of God.

Your lordships must have noticed how in almost every tribute, public or private, from any part of the world which has been paid to His late Majesty the two words have always been combined, respect and affection. I think that there is something very significant in that constant combination. Other monarchs, by their personal charm, sometimes perhaps by their amiable weaknesses, have been regarded with affection. Others by more serious qualities have won respect. For example, in the case of Queen Victoria of ever blessed memory that respect became as her life was prolonged a profound reverence. But to King George respect and affection were given in equal measure, the respect giving depth to the affection, the affection giving warmth to the respect. Let me in a closing moment lay some emphasis upon his steadfast devotion to duty.

I do so because it was revealed in a most moving manner in the very last day of his life. At noon on that day, propped up in his chair, looking so frail and weak, he received his last Privy Council. To the Order constituting a Council of State he gave in his own clear tone the familiar " Approved." Then he made deliberate and repeated efforts, most gallant but most pathetic, to sign his last State paper with his own hand.

Then, when the effort was too great for him, he turned to his Council with a last kindly and kingly smile. My lords, it was a scene which those of us who beheld it will never forget. I hope I have been guilty of no impropriety in describing it. I think it is worthy of record, because it showed that what rallied him in his last conscious hours was this old and undeviating response to the claim of duty.

May I say one word about Her Majesty Queen Mary ? I should like to give my personal testimony to the truly wonderful fortitude and courage which Her Majesty has shown, as I have seen during these last most anxious days. The one who might have been expected to be most overwhelmed was the one from whom to all others surrounding her there radiated calmness and strength. Truly admiration must blend with the sympathy with which she is this day surrounded. We pray with all our hearts that she may be spared to live many years of beneficent activity, to be in ever fuller measure as these years pass the true Queen Mother of her people, and to enjoy her secure possession of their hearts.

I think that the death of King George was singularly fortunate in its time and in its manner—to be spared any lingering weakness, the memory so fresh in his heart of that overflowing gift of the love of his people which he had received. As I looked on his face for the last time on Tuesday morning I saw that there lay upon it a most beautiful tranquillity and peace.

Truly, my lords :

> " Nothing is here for tears, nothing to wail
> Or knock the breast ; no weakness, no contempt,
> Dispraise, or blame ; nothing but well and fair,
> And what may quiet us in a death so noble."

THE HOUSE OF COMMONS

The following speeches were made in the House of Commons on the moving of Addresses to King Edward VIII and Queen Mary :

Mr. BALDWIN.—On occasion there come to us members of the House of Commons these poignant moments that remove us far from the dust and hurly-burly of our daily life and cause us, as it were, to take stock and to remember what we so often forget—that we are representatives here for but a moment of the immemorial procession of the Commons, looking with a proud thankfulness to those who have gone before us and with faith to those who will follow after.

In Westminster Hall, to which we must go in a few moments, I was reminding members of Parliament and members of the Parliaments of the Empire but a few short months ago how in that historic building what has so often been accounted as the first Parliament as we know it was held long years ago ; and it seems to me a curious historical coincidence that some six and three-quarter centuries ago De Montfort summoned that Parliament on the very day of the month that our King departed this life—on January 20. Within a few months De Montfort was dead, defeated and slain as he was in battle, but the ideas that had germinated in his mind were victorious as they never would have been in his life, for, as George Trevelyan said of him, he had made the intellectual conquest of the man who beat him.

The man who beat him was Prince Edward, who became the first, and perhaps the greatest, of that long line of Edwards in English history, the first King who tried to rule through law, and a King of whom one of our greatest historians said : " He saw what was best for his age and for his people. He led the way and he kept the faith." A great tribute to a great king. He, too, was the father of the first Prince of Wales, and his body was laid in that Abbey from which I have just come, having laid to rest a great master of our English tongue and in which building our new King will be crowned with the appropriate pomp and ceremony next year.

From one Edward to another, through the long centuries until yesterday's proclamation of King Edward VIII, the evolution of our Constitution has continued. There have been changes manifold in the usages of Parliament, changes in the nature of the Monarchy, changes even in these last years, but they have been accomplished for the most part without battle, for the most part peacefully and in accordance with the amazing political tradition of our race. The great achievement of the last century, culminating, perhaps, in the reign of King George V, was the coming to terms of democracy and of monarchy, and the system under which we live to-day, a system unique in the world, was evolved. It is a system which, in my belief, gives a stability to the body politic that most countries to-day would give all they have to possess.

How right Bolingbroke was in a flash of inspiration two centuries ago when he remarked that it was far easier to fasten the advantages of a republic on to a monarchy than it was to fasten the advantages of a monarchy on to a republic. The temporal power of the Crown has diminished through the ages, and yet to-day the spiritual power of the Crown is not only far greater than it ever was, but greater than any man, in vision and in dream, could have foreseen it.

It is not only the link that holds together our country ; it holds together the whole Empire of English-speaking peoples. It is, I believe, an indissoluble link, and it holds together the myriad peoples of the East in that great Indian Empire. How has this come about ? It has come about owing to the character of those

who held that great position, the Throne, in the last 100 years—
Queen Victoria, King Edward VII, and King George V. It throws,
as you all know, an infinitely greater responsibility on the Crown
than it ever had in old days. The power of the Crown is not to-day
the power of force. It is a great moral power, and it must depend
on the character and the quality of him who sits upon the Throne.

Important as we may think ourselves, in our generation, who
wrestle with the political problems of the country and act as the
King's advisers, we are but ephemeral compared with the
Monarchy of this country ; and the character of him who sits on
the Throne to-day has this influence for good or ill, not only over
that vast portion of the world which is part of the British Empire,
but, in these days particularly, over the whole world itself.

But it was in the reign of King George V that the greatest and
swiftest changes occurred. And he met the challenge of the times
without flinching, and he triumphed at a time when a slip of
speech even, or of action, might have wrought irreparable damage.
Day by day he discharged those duties which thronged upon him,
with his will rigorously trained to place the public interest first
and last. His own ease and pleasure were never considered. I
cannot tell you how it happened, as you all know it did, but the
sure instinct of our people gradually discerned that whatever
human frailties or limitations might have attached to their King,
his sense of duty to his people amounted to genius.

He communicated his personality by some indefinable,
intangible wave of sympathy and understanding to every one of
his subjects, not only at home but throughout the world. The
messages which have poured into London in these last two days
from all quarters of the globe, from men of high and low estate
and of every creed and colour, testify that the world has lost in his
passing one to whom the world looked up and through whose
example men have led better lives in the accomplishment of their
daily duties and the duties that they do at home and to their
country.

To us, his faithful Commons, there are two things that must be
a great consolation. One is that this great and humble man knew
before his death what his people felt for him, what he never
suspected, but he knew it. The other is that he was taken away
peacefully. He fell asleep with no pain, no suffering, no appre-
hensions, at peace with all the world, and it was not given to him

The final scene in St. George's Chapel, Windsor.

to have that last trial that I think he would have found more difficult to bear than any man I know—having to continue his work with a failing body or possibly with a failing mind. He was taken away from us, delicate it is true, and feeling the effects of that last illness, but with little loss of physical and no loss of mental powers. Those of us whose duty it was to see him frequently have no memory of him but at his best, and his best was something very fine.

Do I need to say a word even to this House of how his power and influence for good were enhanced in a million ways by that rich companionship he shared with the Queen? I said some words in another place about the Queen. I do not wish to say more now, for I feel intensely that her position and her relation with him is something too sacred for us even to comment on in this House. I would merely say that I commend this Resolution, and I assure Her Majesty in commending it that every man and woman in this House, as all the rest of the country, feels a personal sympathy with her at this time—something far removed from conventional grief and conventional sorrow.

But our thoughts, while naturally dwelling on the past, must turn to-day to the future, and we offer respectfully from this House those customary congratulations to our new King as he takes his place in the long line following his distinguished ancestors. No two Sovereigns in that long gallery have had the same countenance or have served their people in identical fashion. The three Sovereigns to whom I have particularly referred to-day were widely divergent in the gifts which they placed upon the common altar of national service. King Edward VIII, in his turn, brings to that same altar a personality richly endowed with experience of public affairs, with the fruits of travel, with universal good will. He has the secret of youth in the prime of age. He has a wider and more intimate knowledge of all classes of his subjects, not only at home but throughout the Dominions and India, than any of his predecessors.

We cannot foresee what path the course of Empire or the course of history may take in the years before us, but our ancient Constitution has shown itself, in the words of his father, " adaptable to change." That virtue has not left it, and while we remain true to our inheritance and to our character it never will. It is now in a special and unique sense in the keeping of the young

King, and we have sworn to serve him and to help him to cherish this great heritage, transmitted and enriched through so many reigns and over so many centuries. Inspired with these memories and endowed as he is, we look forward with confidence and assurance to the new reign, believing that under God's Providence he will establish the Throne more firmly than ever on its surest and only foundation; the hearts of his people.

MR. ATTLEE.—I rise to support on behalf of the Opposition the resolutions which have been so eloquently moved by the Prime Minister. There is to-day no division in this House. We are all united in sorrow at the loss of our great and well-loved Sovereign. We are all animated by the deepest sympathy for the Queen and the Royal Family. But this unity of feeling extends far beyond the bounds of this House. In what we are trying to say here we are wishing to express the feelings of the people of this country whose representatives we are. We know that in every home in the country when the sad news of the death of the King was known there was a sense of personal loss. The whole nation is in mourning. All feel that they have lost a friend.

It has, I think, been given to no previous King to have won such universal affection. No King has ever been able to associate himself so closely with the hopes and fears, with the joys and sorrows of his people. During the Great War, when bereavement visited so many homes, those who had lost their loved ones knew that the King, the Queen, and the Royal Family felt with them in their grief. So it was too in the days of peace when some tragedy, such as a mining disaster, plunged a whole community into mourning. To-day it is the Royal Family which receives the sympathy of the nation.

We know from our own experience how little can be done to give comfort, but in so far as the knowledge that others share their grief can help, the members of the Royal Family are assured that the people of this country, and many millions throughout the world, feel with them. Especially to the Queen in her loneliness do our hearts go out.

The responsibility which rests on the shoulders of the ruler of a great nation must always be heavy, even in times of tranquillity, but when a man is called upon to rule not over one nation but over a commonwealth of nations, not in peace only but during the greatest war in history, not in a period of slow development but when the tide of change is running strongly and old landmarks are being swept away, the burden must be almost intolerable.

Yet this was the lot of King George. He reigned during a period of transition. The short reign of his father as we look back upon it to-day seems but a continuance of the Victorian era. The great changes which were to follow could not then be descried. The forces which for good or evil were to make a new epoch were only beginning to appear. The next twenty-five years saw their rapid development. Even without a world war I think those years must have been years of stress. The advance of science, the spread of education, the progress of ideas of self-government at home and oversea, the pressure of economic forces, must have called for difficult readjustments. The World War came and accelerated all these developments. It was a forcing house of change. The old world passed away and a new one was born.

Two things, I think, were required from the Sovereign of a great State in those conditions. The first was sympathy with the new ideas, and readiness to accept change and to adapt himself to altered conditions ; and the second was the power to give to society, bewildered by the rapid progress of events, a rallying point of stability. These things were found in King George in full measure. They are not common. History affords many instances of rulers who failed, of thrones which have been over-turned because their occupants stubbornly set themselves against the march of events. King George succeeded where others failed because he was a democrat. He was the supreme exponent of the difficult art of constitutional kingship. He knew and understood his people and the age in which they lived, and he progressed with them.

Let me note some outstanding examples. Since 1910 there has been a great extension of democracy in this country. The right to vote has been given to practically every man and woman of full age. The franchise now depends on citizenship and not on the ownership of property. The power of the Upper House has been limited, such a change as elsewhere and at other times had been resisted by monarchs. King George accepted it as a necessary and just consequence of modern conditions. In the same spirit he accepted the achievement of office by a new party the members of which were drawn predominantly from manual workers, an event almost unthinkable only a few decades ago.

He agreed to a series of Acts whereby the Dominions attained equality with the Mother Country. The Irish Free State was created, and India was set on the road to self-government. He relinquished nominal sovereignty, or rather he allowed nominal sovereignty to be apparently diminished, but by doing so he established his real sovereignty in the hearts of the peoples of the Empire. It is the glory of our Constitution that under it great changes, effected elsewhere by violence, are brought about peaceably owing to its adaptability. All this requires that this same quality should be displayed by the King, and this King George did.

Equally important, I think, has been the power of the King to offer a point of stability in a distracted world. The movements of mass hysteria which have been witnessed elsewhere have passed this country by. One reason has been the presence of a King who commanded the respect and affection of his people, who was beyond the spirit of faction, and there has been no need to elevate some individual party leader to a national hero, because the King was there to express the views of his people. King George throughout the long years of the War took his full part in the national effort. His example inspired his people in the struggle. But he was no glorifier of war. He stood always for peace. He sought, as soon as the War was ended, to do his utmost to heal its wounds and recreate good relations between all nations. No less in the difficult post-War years he shared in the work of reconstruction. He was a real social reformer, and took the keenest personal interest in the problems of the day. He recognized the claims of social justice, and felt deeply the tragedy of unemployment. He shared to the full the life of his people.

What were the qualities which enabled the late King to succeed where others have failed? It seems to me that they were his selflessness and devotion to duty, his kindliness and humanity, his practical wisdom, and his courage at all times. The ceremonies which we have witnessed during the last few days carry us back to the times when the functions of a King were very different. The duties of kingship had to be reinterpreted with the passing years. King George showed an incomparable understanding of what was required of a King in the modern world.

It has been a piece of great good fortune for our generation that, just when scientific invention has enabled for the first time so many of the citizens of the British Commonwealth to hear for themselves the voice of their King, we should have had on the Throne a man who so well understood how to speak to his people, a man who set before the nation ideals of peace and justice and service. We have still in our minds his last Christmas message. We have seen the end of a noble life, a life devoted to the welfare of humanity. In the long roll of British Sovereigns none will take a higher place than King George.

We offer our loyal service and congratulations to King Edward VIII, who, as Prince of Wales, has endeared himself to all hearts. He is continuing in a higher sphere and with greater responsibilities the work which he has been doing so well for this country. Like the late King, he showed sympathy with and knowledge of all classes of his subjects, both at home and oversea. He has earned the affection and confidence of all. We know that he will bring to the service of the nation the same great qualities of the mind and heart which his father displayed. May he be spared the same anxieties. The wish of us all is that his reign may be long and prosperous and peaceful.

Sir A. Sinclair.—I rise to support the resolutions and to associate my hon. and right hon. friends and myself with the moving and eloquent speeches in which the Prime Minister and the Leader of the Opposition have expressed the feelings of the House on this melancholy occasion. The King whom we mourn succeeded to a Throne which was already secure in the loyalty and affection and the reverence of the British people. The Throne is no less secure to-day. During a period in which all the institutions of this country and the Empire have been subjected by war and by the processes of rapid change to trials and stresses of almost unexampled severity, he strengthened its hold upon the imagination of the peoples of the British Commonwealth and established it ever more firmly in the hearts of his subjects. To his people of all races, creeds, and languages the King spoke in person as a father to his family, and it is as a father—wise, loving, and dutifully working for the welfare of his family—that we mourn him now and that he will live in our memories hereafter.

But in the midst of our public grief, tempered as it is with gratitude for a life of kingly service and for a shining example of private virtue, we cannot forget the still more poignant and intimate sorrow of those who were nearest to His Majesty, and our hearts go out in true and humble sympathy to our new Sovereign and to the gracious Queen who shared so fully the trials and the achievements of a glorious reign. And with our condolences to the new Sovereign there go, fittingly, our congratulations upon his auspicious accession to the Throne.

Both our natural duty and our loyalty to the memory of the late King alike impel us to rally round his son and to offer in full measure our allegiance and devotion to His Majesty King Edward VIII. The Prime Minister referred to the distinguished and ungrudging services which His Majesty has already rendered to this country and his Empire. Conviction must have been borne in upon the House that perhaps never in our history has a Prince ascended the Throne so fully equipped to bear the glorious burden of Sovereignty.

We remember also with what zeal he has followed the lead of his august father in his concern for the welfare of the poorest of his people and of the victims of war, economic depression and unemployment. He has both earnestly commended to others and constantly practised himself the ideals of social service and fellowship. The gracious Message he has sent to us to-day is eloquent in its simplicity and directness of the sincerity of his feelings and of his loyalty to the noble traditions of his family. So it is our confident hope, as it is our fervent prayer, that the reign which is now beginning will be long and prosperous and add yet another honourable chapter to the chronicles of an illustrious house.

———◆———

TO THE CHILDREN

Mr. O. F. Morshead, King's Librarian at Windsor Castle, in a broadcast to children, said :

For those who were privileged to share the late King's friendship the present seems a moment for reticence, when the springs of feeling and the instincts of restraint combine to hamper thought and expression. But if there is indeed a duty to break silence it is surely towards the schoolchildren, to whom the King himself

King Edward VIII sprinkles earth on his father's coffin.

A part of the vast array of flowers sent to Windsor.

directed a thought at the very height of his Jubilee celebrations, only a few months ago. He loved children, as the greatest men so often do ; and so I will try to tell you about some of the fine personal characteristics which underlay the robes and trappings of State.

Not that you do not know him already. None of you who heard his rare but perfect broadcast talks can say that he did not know the man behind that resonant, honest voice. In addresses free from affectation, strong, clear, friendly, the King stood by your fireside, as clearly revealed as if you had been standing by his. And some children there are who *have* stood by his fireside in his Norfolk home, because every year he used to give a prize to some selected candidate from one of the local schools ; and if one of those boys or girls were here at the microphone now instead of me this is the account he could give you. He would say :

" I was shown up into the King's study, quite a small room, and there was the King standing on the hearthrug, and shaking hands with me, and talking just as if he'd known me all my life. I was ever so frightened before I went in, but the funny thing was that directly he started talking I felt as if *I'd* known *him* all my life. He asked all about home, and whether any of our people were out of work, and whether I was as proud of being a Norfolk person as he was, and a whole lot of other things ; and it seemed all the time as if he really wanted to know. And while he was talking I looked round at the rather hard-looking red leather chairs, and the grey parrot on a stand, which seemed fond of him, and the little dog which was looking up at him, and the neat pile of books on the low table by his chair, and a lot of scarlet dispatch-boxes—one of them was open, and a great big paper was lying on it, which he had been reading when I came in.

" Presently he took up a Bible, saying that that was what he was going to give me, but before doing it he wanted to tell me a story. ' When I was your age,' he said, ' my grandmother (she was Queen Victoria, you know) gave me a Bible, and she advised me to read a chapter in it every night. I have always done it, wherever I have been—except, of course, during that bad illness ; I couldn't do it then. Now *you* can do as you like. But if you make that a rule of your life, and stick to it, I don't think you'll regret it when you come to my age . . . and you've got a long way to go yet.' And then he laughed his great boyish laugh, and I came away."

Now that story, which is true, will tell you nearly everything that I have to say. He was, at whatever angle you met him, a profoundly modest man. Most of the biggest men are. He was only proud about two things ; he was proud of the antiquity of his kingly office, and he was very proud of his birthright as an Englishman, like us. We have our loyalty to our home in earliest years, to our school, our team, our firm, our regiment, our families, as the years pass ; and, above all, we think of loyalty in terms of the respect which we owe to the Sovereign. He had his loyalty, too—towards you and me. He was worried about those who, through no fault of their own, are out of work, and about all those who must bear into an uncharted future the scars and bereavements of the Great War. He did not bear such sorrows as these, and many others, lightly ; and by the perpetual nature of his office they were always before him.

His heart was no less in all our manly amusements and recreations. He had himself sailed his famous old yacht Britannia for over forty summers ; he sailed her for all she was worth (which was a lot), glowing at her successes, and never cast down by defeat. He had never been up in an aeroplane, and is probably the last King of whom that will be said. At shooting his mastery was as evident as his unselfishness. " I knew you wouldn't want the best stand every time, Sir," said an old friend with whom he was staying, " I said you'd prefer to draw lots like the rest of us." Nothing could better illustrate the cordial terms upon which the King established himself among the host of friends whom he gathered round him—and whom he never forgot.

At racing he was a great deal more knowledgeable than his rather meagre successes might imply ; but he refused to accept defeat, and to the end took a lively interest in all that concerned the Turf. You will perhaps enter more into his absorbing preoccupation with postage stamps, in which field his collection is, I believe, without serious rival. You will not be surprised when I tell you that they are all British ; and there is little indeed that he did not himself know about them. He used to declare that they had saved his life in the War ; for during such intervals as he could spare from his constant and anxious duties he would obtain complete relaxation poring over some rare issue with the aid of a magnifying glass.

His happy nature was seen at its best as host, whether at Windsor or at his beloved Sandringham. He was bent upon giving everybody else a good time, and he never tired of recounting his inexhaustible memories of the men and events with which, in the course of his long public life, he had been connected. He was, in fact, though he never seemed aware of it, a wonderfully gifted conversationalist, with an alert sense of fun. The kindest of men himself, his talk, for all its liveliness, was never ill-natured ; and if he mentioned people's foibles, as he occasionally did, it was only in a vein of appreciative and whimsical humour. As good people do, he put everyone at their best ; and he carried friendliness and merriment with him into any assemblage.

You will have read in the morning paper the moving words which His present Majesty addressed to the Privy Council. I read them in the train, coming up from Windsor ; and as we sped on through the grey countryside my thoughts travelled back to the same hour last Tuesday at Sandringham. We had been out for a walk through those beautiful woodlands, sunny and still, the King on Jock, his little fat white pony, the Queen and some others accompanying him on foot. On our return he dismounted at the garden gates, close by the little church where he is lying at this minute, and Jock rubbed his head against his master for the carrots which he knew were coming. It happens that I had brought for the King a new acquisition, the original handwritten document from which the girl Queen Victoria had read her speech to the Privy Council on the morrow of William IV's death. It had strayed into private possession, and now its loyal owner had asked me to offer it to His Majesty. As we walked back to the house he was telling me of the insupportable emotion with which he had himself confronted the Privy Council when his own turn came ; how he had been up all night, and could hardly snatch the time next morning to jot down the notes of what he wanted to say. Perfectly devoted to his father, he despaired in his affliction of ever being able to give utterance to his thoughts. Now, within one brief week, the cycle is complete.

That evening at dinner as usual among his guests and household, his natural gaiety reasserted itself. " How many woodcock did *you* shoot to-day ? " he asked one of them—and then, quick as a flash, " And how many did you miss ? " It was just a flicker of the old flame, stirring among the embers. Only a week ago.

I have tried to show you how warmly human was the latest King to join the pageant of our long past. I should like to end by reminding you of the words which Shakespeare puts into the mouth of one of his predecessors, King Richard II :

> How can you say to me, I am a King ?
> For you have but mistook me all this while :
> I live with bread like you, feel want,
> Taste grief, need friends . . .
> For within the hollow crown
> That rounds the mortal temples of a King
> Keeps Death his court, and there the antic sits,
> Scoffing his state, and grinning at his pomp ;
> Allowing him a breath, a little scene
> To monarchise, be fear'd, and kill with looks ; . . .
> As if this flesh which walls about our life
> Were brass impregnable ; and humour'd thus
> Comes at the last and with a little pin
> Bores through his castle wall, and farewell King !

———◆———

FROM THE UNITED STATES

Mr. Raymond Swing paid the following tribute to King George in the transatlantic bulletin broadcast by the B.B.C. on January 24 :

You will have already heard in your newspapers of the national sympathy with which this country has shared with the British people the loss of their Sovereign. That sympathy has had the fullest formal expression, but it has voiced itself informally too —much more eloquently and deeply than was required by mere courtesy and regard.

Our newspapers have devoted as much space to the death of King George as to a great domestic event, some of the New York papers publishing three or four, or even more, pages of news and comments daily throughout the week. George V has been the subject of thousands of editorial eulogies, many of them hailing him as a wise and great King. The warmth of the admiration and the extent of the knowledge of British affairs and of the King's part in them would have surprised many of you. And it brought home to me how much wider is the influence of a British Monarch to-day—how much more pervading his personality—than ever before in the history of Kings.

King George, of course, was known in a way and in a measure not accorded to Sovereigns in the past. There are millions of homes in the United States where his physical voice has been heard, and where, by his gift of simple, dignified expression, he has raised up a definite sense of personal reality and presence in the minds of his listeners.

To this knowledge of him the news reels and moving pictures added the visual dimension of the man. To us he was an individual known, admired, and respected, and when he died millions of people in America were moved by more than the tragic drama of a change of rulers in a foreign land. They were identified with the man, and could feel his loss as the departure of someone personally known.

This intimacy with the King, made possible through modern invention, was still greater, of course, in Great Britain, where the King was both the man and a symbol of national unity. But it is well to recognize that he had an intimate following in this country that no foreign personage has had before.

His words to the Empire in your Christmas celebration just a few weeks ago entered countless homes in America. I know in my own home—the hour was towards the end of the forenoon—and we had gone all round the Empire with the B.B.C. engineers, and waited, all of us, a little impatiently, to hear the King. And as he spoke a silence fell on us all, and we were touched, not because we heard the voice of the British Sovereign, but, first of all, because he was such a human man, speaking humanly of human things.

The rapt interest with which we are following the news from England this week would tempt anyone, I think, to call attention to the peculiarly intimate association of our two nations. This is something which many persons would like—so very much like— to engender, and for quite obviously good reasons ; and much is said about it and its desirability which sometimes seems a little beside the point, since intimate association and a sense of its value are not to be had by exhortations and arguments.

M

People don't come to like each other, or feel close to each other through exercising their logic. Such a feeling builds up beneath the conscious mind, and then through some happening it expresses itself, so that consciously one is made aware of it. And that feeling has expressed itself this week, not in a way to astonish anyone who knows the two countries intimately but vividly enough to confirm any hope one might have had for it.

There is in this country without any doubt underneath the surface of current doings and controversies a sense of fraternity with the British nation, and without any doubt this is not felt in anything like the same degree for any other people. This is not to say that this emotional subconscious sense is going to wipe away surface controversies, for it is not. You have your national life, and we have ours, and they are separate, and inevitably competitive in many of the secondary marches of life.

This is not the occasion to hold forth on the theme of Anglo-American friendship, and I raise the subject at this time only to say that George V, by being the man he was, and Edward VIII, by being the man he is—men intimately appraised, and accepted and liked, as men can be in this century by far-away countries—have contributed much to that underlying feeling. And the death of the King has given expression to it in a notable and memorable way.

After the hush of the events of this week have passed we shall again go our own separate ways, and we shall speak out in criticism, and sometimes even reproach, about each other, but we shall not be able to ignore or minimize the underlying fact of the intimacy which has been revealed this week.

CHAPTER VI

BIOGRAPHY

BORN at Marlborough House on June 3, 1865, Prince George Frederick Ernest Albert was the second son of King Edward VII and Queen Alexandra (then Prince and Princess of Wales). From an early age he and his elder brother, the Duke of Clarence, born in 1864, were placed under the tutorship of the Rev. J. N. (afterwards Canon) Dalton, then curate of Sandringham, under whose supervision they received an excellent all-round education. Prince George is described as being brimming over with good spirits and fun in those days. King Edward, one of the shrewdest and most sagacious of men, was convinced that the Royal Navy " affords the very best possible training for any boy," and so the two Princes went to the Britannia, as naval cadets, two days after Prince George's twelfth birthday. They passed through the ordinary course and joined the Bacchante in August, 1879, for a cruise to the West Indies, in the course of which, on January 8, 1880, they were rated midshipmen. The Bacchante was a fully rigged cruiser-corvette, as fine as any then afloat.

While in the Bacchante the Princes, except that they slept in cots under the poop and were not required to keep the middle watch, were treated exactly as the other youngsters, and carried out all the regular drills and duties in all weathers, and by night as well as by day. After a month at home in 1880 the Princes rejoined their ship and made a prolonged cruise, in the course of which they visited South America, South Africa, Australia, the Fiji Islands, Japan, Ceylon, Egypt, Palestine, and Greece. It was the first of a series of voyages which made the younger Prince the most travelled of all English Sovereigns, save, possibly, his own eldest son and successor.

The published " Cruise of the Bacchante " does not throw much light upon the personal adventures and impressions of Prince George as distinct from those of his brother. Mr. Dalton, the editor, succeeded in almost entirely merging the two very different individualities of the Princes. Only occasionally are the brothers allowed to appear singly in the long chronicle. We are told, however, under date of January 22, 1880, that " George only weighs 88lb. and is 4ft. 10⅜in. high. Thanks to gymnastics his arm is nearly as thick as his brother's. He is nearly an inch taller than the Duke of Edinburgh was at the same age in 1858."

The book depicts Prince George as a sportsman and a lover of adventure. Such was, throughout, his character. His reputation in the Navy was always that of " a good sort," and his devotion to all the pursuits which are followed by healthy young Englishmen was in itself sufficient to ensure his popularity among his fellow-officers. Year by year he strengthened the ties which bound him to his first profession. On May 1, 1883, after a few months on the Continent, he was appointed to the corvette Canada, and in her served part of a commission on the North America and West Indies Station. In 1884, having been made a sub-lieutenant on his nineteenth birthday, he came home to study at the Royal Naval College, Greenwich, where he gained a first-class in seamanship, torpedo work, and gunnery, and on October 8, 1885, he was promoted lieutenant. In this capacity he was appointed on January 14, 1886, to the Thunderer, in the Mediterranean Squadron, and was subsequently transferred to the Dreadnought. He had already, in 1884, been raised to the dignity of a Knight of the Garter, and while in the Dreadnought he was, on June 21, 1887, appointed Personal Naval Aide-de-Camp to the Queen. In 1888, still remaining in the Mediterranean, he joined the Alexandra, flagship of his uncle, the late Duke of Edinburgh.

Prince George quitted the Alexandra on February 1, 1889, on appointment to the Northumberland, flagship in the Channel, and during the summer of the same year, when the German Emperor with his fleet visited Spithead, he received his first independent command of Torpedo-boat No. 79, in which he subsequently took part in the naval manoeuvres, and attracted attention by a smart piece of seamanship in towing into port under great diffi-culties another torpedo-boat which had been disabled in a storm. It is of this time in his naval career that the story is told of how the late Sir Edmund Commerell sent for Prince George and told him that his father wished to see him at Goodwood. " But, Sir," said the lieutenant, " what is to become of my torpedo-boat ? " The Admiral suggested that he thought he might be spared for the day,

King George as a child with his brother, the Duke of Clarence, and his sisters (left to right) the Princess Royal (Duchess of Fife), Queen Maud of Norway, and Princess Victoria.

Two early photographs of King George in naval uniform.

to which the Prince replied : " No, Sir ; I have orders to take this boat to sea, and go I must." Whereupon he steamed out to Spithead in an easterly gale.

On appointment to the Royal yacht Osborne in September, 1889, the Prince began a course of gunnery, in which he always took great interest, in the Excellent at Portsmouth. He was now in his twenty-fifth year, and was still only a lieutenant. It is said to have been owing to the wise advice of the Duke of Edinburgh that his nephew was not promoted in the Jubilee year. The Duke himself had been too early advanced.

Instead, therefore, of being made a commander, Prince George was offered a command as a lieutenant, and, on May 6, 1890, commissioned the first-class gunboat Thrush, in which, soon afterwards, he joined the squadron on the North American and the West Indies Station. The Thrush, after little more than a year, was recalled to England, and the Prince brought her home, and on August 24, 1891, paid her off at Chatham. It was after his return from this cruise that he was promoted commander.

By the death of the Duke of Clarence on January 14, 1892, the whole prospects of Prince George were changed, and his hope of further advancement in the active ranks of his profession was necessarily abandoned. He commanded, indeed, the cruiser Melampus in the manoeuvres of that year, and six years later hoisted his pennant on board the Crescent for a cruise of about eleven weeks. On each occasion his renewed association with the sea service was extremely popular, and the tone of his ship and her state of discipline elicited commendation from the older officers. He was promoted Captain in 1893, Rear-Admiral in 1901, Vice-Admiral in 1903, Admiral in 1907, and Admiral of the Fleet in May, 1910.

In May, 1892, Prince George was created Duke of York, Earl of Inverness and Baron Killarney, and on July 6, 1893, he was married at the Chapel Royal, St. James's, to Princess Victoria Mary, daughter of the Duke of Teck and Princess Mary, sister of the old Duke of Cambridge, so long Commander-in-Chief of the Army. The Princess had previously been betrothed to the Duke of Clarence. The wedding was celebrated as a public holiday, although not proclaimed as such in most parts of the Empire.

The next seven exacting years were filled with the round of ceremonial. In all these duties the Duchess took her place by her husband's side, and as the years went on, as Princess of Wales, and finally as Queen Consort—the first of British birth since Anne, the Queen of James II—she won, by her sheer goodness and the quick responsiveness of her feelings, not merely the respect but the deep affection of the whole nation.

On June 23, 1894, the Prince of Wales, was born, and was christened Edward Albert Christian George Andrew Patrick David. A second Prince, whom we now know as the Duke of York, was born on December 14, 1895, and was christened Albert Frederick Arthur George. In 1897 and 1900 their marriage was blessed with further children, Princess Mary, now Countess of Harewood, and Prince Henry, Duke of Gloucester, and in 1902 Prince George, Duke of Kent, was born. In 1905 came the youngest, Prince John, whose death at the age of 13 was a sad loss to his parents and to his brothers and sister.

The Commonwealth of Australia came into being on January 1, 1901. In the previous summer Queen Victoria commissioned the Duke of York to open the first Session of the Australian Parliament in her name. In touching words her Majesty explained that she naturally shrank from parting with Her grandson for so long a period. But rising, as she ever did, to the greatness of the occasion, she recognized the paramount desirability of the sacrifice. In the midst of the preparations for departure Queen Victoria died. But she had been so much interested in the Duke of York's mission that it was decided, nevertheless, to carry out her wishes. This memorable tour started from Portsmouth on March 16, 1901, and ended on November 1, after a journey ot over 50,000 miles, of which over 38,000 miles were on board the liner Ophir. The detailed record of such figures, down to the very number of handshakes, was duly published in the resulting volume, "The Web of Empire"; it was highly typical of the King's lifelong devotion to statistics and method.

At Melbourne, on May 9, the Duke opened the first Federal Parliament of Australia amid scenes of the utmost enthusiasm. Visits were paid to Brisbane and Sydney. Thence the Ophir proceeded to Auckland, where the Royal party took a deep interest in the Maoris and their customs, and the outward journey concluded with visits to Wellington, Christchurch, and Dunedin. On the return voyage the journey was broken at Hobart, Adelaide, Albany, and Perth. From Fremantle a course was steered for

Mauritius, and thence to Durban and Capetown. Another long sea stretch brought the party to Quebec, whence Canada was crossed to Vancouver, by way of Ottawa. On the return trip from Victoria, the westernmost point of the journey, reached on October 1, Niagara Falls were visited, and the homeward voyage was from Halifax, touching at St. John's, Newfoundland.

A speech which stirred the country was made by the Prince at a Guildhall luncheon on December 5, 1901. After describing his Colonial tour and the enthusiasm with which he and his consort had been received at every stage, the Prince said :

If I were asked to specify any particular impressions derived from our journey, I should unhesitatingly place before all others that of loyalty to the Crown and of attachment to the Old Country ; and it was touching to hear the invariable references to home even from the lips of those who never had been, or were ever likely to be, in these islands. And with this loyalty were unmistakable evidences of the consciousness of strength, a consciousness of a true and living membership in the Empire, and a consciousness of power and readiness to share the burden and responsibility of that membership.

The events of thirteen years later were to show how accurately the Prince had appreciated the spirit of the peoples of the Empire. Further, the Prince brought a message of grave importance to the comfortable, easy-going England of those days. He said :

To the distinguished representatives of the commercial interests of the Empire, whom I have the pleasure of seeing here to-day, I venture to allude to the impression which seemed generally to prevail among their brethren across the seas, that the Old Country must wake up if she intends to maintain her old position of pre-eminence in her Colonial trade against foreign competitors.

" Wake up, England ! " The cry at the moment electrified those who heard it, and the voice of her Prince who had seen for himself and knew whereof he spoke, had undoubtedly a lasting effect. All over the country, in office and factory, in counting-house and mine, his blunt phrase aroused heart-searchings which bore fruit in renewed effort for the national prosperity.

The relations between Great Britain and Germany were none too pleasant in 1902. The German Press throughout the South

African War was vituperative, and a speech made by Mr. Chamberlain, largely misunderstood in Germany, led to a storm of indignation there. In the midst of an awkward situation the Prince of Wales visited Berlin, in January, 1902, in order to take part in the celebration of the Emperor William's birthday. The visit was regarded in this country as wholly devoid of political meaning, but the cordial reception of the Prince by the Emperor was reflected in a noticeable improvement in the tone of the more respectable organs of the German Press. The remainder of this year, as also 1903, was spent by the Prince mainly in ceremonial duties, and King Edward's illness immediately before the date fixed for the Coronation naturally threw upon him a great increase of work owing to the presence in London of representatives of the Colonies and India.

In the winter of 1905-06 their Royal Highnesses visited India, sailing in H.M.S. Renown. Some 9,000 miles were travelled by rail in little over four months, and twenty-eight nights were spent in the train. A week was passed in Egypt on the way home. The King and Queen met the Prince and Princess at Corfu, and, with King George of Greece, accompanied them to Athens. On their return the Prince, at Guildhall, on May 17, again gave an account of his tour. In India, he said, although he and the Princess had been welcomed everywhere by holiday-making crowds, they did not forget the misery and poverty which existed in the famine districts through which they passed. He had been impressed by the loyalty and personal allegiance to the Crown of the great feudatory Princes, their nobility of mind, and the great powers which they possessed for doing good. Finally, he revealed his insight into a grave problem in the words :

I cannot help thinking from all I have heard and seen that the task of governing India will be made the easier if we, on our part, infuse into it a wider element of sympathy. I will venture to predict that to such sympathy there will be an ever-abundant and genuine response. May we not also hope for a still fuller measure of trust and confidence in our earnest desire and efforts to promote the well-being and to further the best interests of every class ?

In 1908 the Prince paid his sixth visit to Canada, this time for the tercentenary celebration of the founding of Quebec. The nine days' visit was a great success. On the way home his ship,

King George and Queen Mary photographed with the bridesmaids, after their wedding at St. James's Palace on July 6, 1893.

A photograph taken during the Coronation Service in Westminster Abbey. (From the Sir Benjamin Stone Collection in the Birmingham Reference Library.)

the Indomitable, the largest and most modern of cruisers, made a record run of 2,880 miles in five days eighteen hours forty minutes, the Prince himself going down into the stokehold and doing a little stoking " for luck."

Never were his qualities of sincerity, simplicity and manliness more transparently displayed than on the death of King Edward VII on May 6, 1910. It is no secret that between father and son, unlike as they were in many ways, there had subsisted a degree of mutual understanding and a warmth of affection for which the past history of the relations between Monarch and Heir had afforded no parallel. Every morning the Prince of Wales would call at the Palace and remain with King Edward in close and prolonged consultation upon the affairs of the day. And the respect thus engendered for the views and outlook of his father sank deep into the Prince, and remained a profound influence to the end.

In a message to the Navy, issued on May 10, the King, after expressing his gratitude for its faithful and distinguished services to his " beloved father," said :

Educated and trained in that profession which I love so dearly, retirement from active duty has in no sense diminished my feelings of affection for it. For thirty-three years I have had the honour of serving in the Navy, and such intimate participation in its life and work enables me to know how thoroughly I can depend upon that spirit of loyalty and zealous devotion to duty of which the glorious history of the Navy is the outcome.

That you will ever continue to be, as in the past, the foremost defender of your country's honour, I know full well, and your fortunes will always be followed by me with deep feelings of pride and affectionate interest.

To his people the King wrote :

The voice of affection and of loving devotion to the memory of my dear father which has come from every part of the Empire, the outward public demonstrations, especially those in the Capital during the two stages of his passing to his last resting-place, and the pathetic manner in which vast multitudes of his loving subjects patiently and reverently awaited opportunity to pay a last tribute to his memory, have profoundly touched me and my whole family.

A sorrow so sudden and unlooked-for might well have been over-whelming. But the sentiments evoked by it have made me realize that it is a loss common to me and to my people ; they share it with me. I do not stand alone.

With such thoughts I take courage, and hopefully look into the future, strong in my faith in God, trusting my people, and cherishing the Laws and Constitutions of my beloved country.

At King Edward's death there were some who thought that the country would have a Court less sympathetic towards the joyous side of life—high-minded and worthy indeed, but lacking some-thing of the social brilliance that had blossomed after the death of Queen Victoria. In so far as such doubts represented a fear that the new King and Queen, whose pure and happy domestic life was universally recognized, would be indifferent to popular pleasures, they were soon to prove unfounded. It was with real enjoyment that the King throughout his reign attended the theatre, race meetings, and other places of recreation, but his greatest pleasure was game shooting. He was indeed one of the finest game shots in the kingdom—probably the finest after the death of Lord Ripon.

During the first few months of the reign a foolish legend was in circulation to the effect that His Majesty during the lifetime of his elder brother had been morganatically married at Malta to the daughter of a naval officer. The matter was brought to a head by the trial, in February, 1911, of Edward F. Mylius, a friend of and fellow-worker with a notorious Indian agitator, Krish-navarma, for publishing a criminal libel on the King in a periodical called the *Liberator*, in which the charge of bigamy and desertion was made in the most circumstantial manner. The Attorney-General had no difficulty in proving beyond the faintest shadow of doubt that the whole story was a string of fabrications, and the Lord Chief Justice sentenced the prisoner to the maximum penalty of twelve months' imprisonment. After sentence had been passed, the Attorney-General read the following document :

I am authorized by His Majesty to state publicly that he was never married, except to the Queen, and that he never went through any ceremony of marriage except with the Queen ; and, further, that he would have attended to give evidence to this effect had he not received advice from the Law Officers of the Crown that it would be unconstitutional for him to do so.

The Coronation took place amid scenes of splendour on June 22, 1911. Every phase of our national life was represented in the 8,000 persons for whom seats were provided in the Abbey. Indian Princes in their rich and picturesque costumes brought the homage of our great Dependency ; the five self-governing Dominions sent their Prime Ministers ; every civilized State was represented, according to its form of government, either by someone near to the Throne or by a man eminently distinguished by the suffrages of his countrymen.

It was observed that, departing from the precedent of King Edward's Coronation, the Archbishop of Canterbury crowned both the King and the Queen ; and it was observed also that the crowns themselves were new, and that while that of the Queen contained the Koh-i-noor, the King's Imperial Crown bore, together with the ruby of Agincourt, the great diamond which had been presented to King Edward by the Government of South Africa. Such a juxtaposition seemed to symbolize at once both the continuity of the monarchy and the unity of the Empire. The celebrations extended over several weeks ; and on July 1 was published a message from the King to his people, thanking them for their affectionate demonstrations of loyalty, and concluding with the words :

Believing that this generous and outspoken sympathy with the Queen and myself is, under God, our surest source of strength, I am encouraged to go forward with renewed hope. Whatever perplexities or difficulties may lie before me and my people, we shall all unite in facing them resolutely, calmly and with public spirit, confident that under Divine guidance, the ultimate outcome will be to the common good.

Of the subsequent State visits of the King and Queen to Dublin, Wales, and Edinburgh, it need only be said that they were eminently successful. At Caernarvon the happy idea of a public installation of the young Prince of Wales was carried out with charming picturesqueness.

The first year of the King's reign was one of great anxieties. The action of Germany with regard to Morocco brought the peace of Europe into serious danger, and though the peril was averted by an agreement between France and Germany, a haunting sense remained that the relations between England and Germany were not satisfactory. After the Coronation, too, a sort of epidemic of unrest broke out in many of the great cities and ports, and in August a dock strike in London threw 100,000 men idle. The unrest spread, and culminated in the most extensive railway strike that the country had ever known.

Nor was the situation brighter in the sphere of politics. The Government had determined to " deal with " the House of Lords. At the height of the struggle King Edward died. The feeling that his successor must not be plunged at once into a constitutional struggle led to a temporary truce. The Parliament Bill, announced in King George's Speech from the Throne on February 6, 1911, as intended for " settling the relations between the two Houses of Parliament with the object of securing the more effective working of the Constitution," was substantially identical with the Bill of 1910. The real agitation did not begin until the Lords had read the Bill a third time with various important amendments. The effect of the chief of these, proposed by Lord Lansdowne, would have been to spoil the Home Rule scheme.

The sequel was Mr. Asquith's announcement that the King would be advised to exercise his prerogative, in other words, to create sufficient Liberal Peers to secure the passing into law of the Bill in substantially the same form as that in which it left the House of Commons, and His Majesty had been pleased to signify that he would consider it his duty to accept and act on that advice. On July 24 the Unionist leaders were received in audience by the King, and on the following day Lord Lansdowne advised his followers to give way, " as they were no longer free agents." In the division which followed Lord Lansdowne and some 240 peers abstained from voting, and the resolution for accepting the original Bill, with one or two minor concessions, was carried by a majority of seventeen.

It must have been with a sense of relief that the King on November 11, 1911, left the scene of all these controversies and, with the Queen, took ship in the Medina for India. It was the first time that a British Sovereign had left these islands in order to do honour by his presence to a country which is an integral part of the British Empire.

On December 7, amid scenes for which there was no precedent in the long history of Asia, the King-Emperor and his Consort made their State entry into the Imperial city of Delhi. They were received at the Salimgarh Bastion by the Governor-General and

King George shaking hands with Marshal Foch during a visit to Paris.

Placing a wreath on the Cross of Sacrifice
in Terlincthun War Cemetery.

With Earl Haig (then Sir Douglas Haig)
in France during the War,

all the great officials of India ; they walked in procession into the
fort, where the Princes and Chiefs of India were presented ; they
traversed the whole length of the city, receiving the homage of
multitudes of their Indian subjects, and finally, on the summit of
the famous Ridge at a spot for ever hallowed in British annals,
they were loyally welcomed by the chosen representatives of
British India.

The Durbar, one of the most gorgeous and significant ceremonies that the world has ever seen, was held on December 12.
From first to last it assumed the character of a solemn rite
performed with stately and almost sacramental fervour in the
presence of 100,000 people. Their Majesties were seated on
thrones in the pavilion, in full view of multitudes of people, when
the Delhi Herald read a Proclamation announcing His Majesty's
Coronation. This was followed by the announcement by the
Governor-General of " the customary grants, concessions, reliefs,
and benefactions " which the King-Emperor had been " graciously
pleased to bestow upon this glorious and memorable occasion."
They included the immediate devotion of 50 lakhs of rupees to the
promotion of popular education, and the extension of the Victoria
Cross to the native officers, non-commissioned officers, and men
of the Indian Army.

Then, to the astonishment of the company, for the secret had
been singularly well kept, the King-Emperor, taking a paper from
the Governor-General, read in a clear voice the announcement of
two momentous changes—the transfer of the capital to Delhi, and
the practical reversal of the partition of Bengal. Three days later
His Majesty laid the first stones of the new Imperial capital. As
he took the trowel in his hand and ran his eye along one of the
stones he was heard to remark that the stone did not seem to him
quite straight. His Majesty's keen eye had not deceived him. The
stone, which had not then been finally adjusted, was slightly out
of alignment, but the fault was immediately corrected.

Two comparatively quiet years followed, though the clouds
were obviously growing. In the April of 1914 the King and Queen
paid a State visit to President Poincaré, a visit which gave a new
sense of the vital consequences of the Entente. But that bugbear
of British politics, the question of Home Rule, still occupied major
attention. There were deplorable incidents at home and in Ireland
—altercations in the House of Commons, the Curragh crisis, and

the landing of arms by the Ulster Volunteer Force. Matters were fast reaching a deadlock when *The Times* startled the political world by announcing that the King had summoned a Conference of two representatives of each of the four parties to the controversy, under the chairmanship of the Speaker, to meet at Buckingham Palace. His Majesty opened the Conference with a gravely-worded speech, in which he spoke of the cry of civil war being on the lips of the most responsible and sober-minded of the people. The Conference held four meetings, but failed to agree, either in principle or in detail, upon a definition of the area to be excluded from the Home Rule Bill.

In the middle of that crisis suddenly came the War. The King had up to the last been striving to avert the catastrophe. He sent a message to the Emperor William by Prince Henry of Prussia, and in reply to the latter's telegram proposing that he should use his influence on France and Russia that they should remain neutral, he telegraphed :

Please assure William that I am doing all I can, and will continue to do all that lies in my power, to maintain the peace of Europe.

To the Tsar he telegraphed, on August 1, a personal appeal " to remove the misapprehension which I feel must have occurred, and to leave still open grounds for negotiation and possible peace." The Tsar answered that he would gladly have accepted his proposals had not the German Government declared war that very afternoon. A telegram to the Emperor William of the same date was equally without avail.

From August 4 an entire change passed over the activities of King and people. To Admiral Jellicoe and his officers and men the King sent

the assurance of my confidence that under your direction they will receive and renew the old glories of the Royal Navy, and prove once again the sure shield of Britain and of her Empire in the hour of trial.

In the message issued early in September to the Dominions the King made the following fine declaration of principle and policy :

Had I stood aside when, in defiance of pledges to which my kingdom was a party, the soil of Belgium was violated and her cities laid desolate, when the very life of the French nation was threatened with extinction,

174

I should have sacrificed my honour and given to destruction the liberties of my Empire and of mankind.

On November 29 the King left for the Front. His Majesty was enthusiastically welcomed by the troops, both British and Indian, and the French soldiers and the population through whom he passed during his stay were almost equally delighted. For nearly a week the King lived at Headquarters, having frequent conferences with Sir John French, carefully inspecting both the fighting lines and the wounded, and witnessing some artillery attacks upon the enemy's trenches. He took the opportunity of investing the King of the Belgians with the Order of the Garter. Visits to the Grand Fleet followed in February and March, 1915.

Ever ready to sacrifice himself, even in minor matters, for the public good, the King wrote to the Chancellor of the Exchequer that " if it were deemed advisable he would be prepared to set the example by giving up all alcoholic liquor himself and issuing orders against its consumption in the Royal Household." His Majesty's letter, which was followed on April 6 by the issue of the orders in question, received an immediate voluntary response from the country and Empire.

Another visit to the Grand Fleet in July preceded a number of tours of munition factories. The recruiting question reached its critical point in October with the introduction of the Derby scheme. The final efforts of the voluntary system to provide the requisite numbers of men for the Army received a great stimulus from an appeal from the King to his people, published on October 23.

At this moment the King was in France on another visit to the Army, which, unhappily, was marred and ended by a serious accident. In the midst of an inspection of the troops on October 28 the King's horse, frightened by the cheers of the men, reared twice, slipped on the greasy road, and fell upon its rider, pinning him down. The King was severely bruised and suffered much pain, but no bones were broken. It was many weeks before he had entirely recovered. Meanwhile, before leaving for England on November 1, he issued a special Order of the Day to the troops, in the course of which he said :

I have decorated many of you. But had I decorated all who deserve recognition for conspicuous valour, there would have been no limit, for the whole Army is illustrious. It is the dogged determination evinced by all ranks which will at last bring you to victory. Keep the goal in sight, and remember it is the final lap that wins.

The most striking incident of the first few months of 1915, filled as they were with the works of sympathy, encouragement, and kindness to which the King and Queen never failed to devote themselves, was His Majesty's gift to the Exchequer of £100,000, to be applied in whatever manner was deemed best by the Government—a truly Royal example of patriotic desire to sacrifice personal wealth for public purposes, which has been repeatedly followed both during and after the War.

On May 31 came the naval battle off the coast of Jutland. In reply to a birthday message from Admiral Jellicoe on behalf of the Grand Fleet, the King wrote that he was deeply touched, and added :

It reached me on the morrow of a battle which has once more displayed the splendid gallantry of the officers and men under your command.

I mourn the loss of brave men, many of them personal friends of my own, who have fallen in their country's cause. Yet even more do I regret that the German High Sea Fleet, in spite of its heavy losses, was enabled by the misty weather to evade the full consequences of an encounter they have always professed to desire, but for which, when the opportunity arrived, they showed no inclination.

Early in June the King visited the Grand Fleet, and addressed representatives of its various units on parade.

On the eve of the third year of the War the King expressed the national determination in a message, dated " Midnight, August 3," addressed to the Heads and Sovereigns of Allied States, and in another to the King of the Belgians. To the Sovereigns and Heads of the Allied States he wrote :

I feel assured that you are in accord with me in the determination that the sacrifices which our valiant troops have so nobly made shall not have been offered in vain, and that the liberties for which they are fighting shall be fully guaranteed and secured.

In August he paid another visit, which lasted a week, to the Army in France and inspected everything—trenches, captured dug-outs, batteries, and prisoners ; his days were spent strenuously,

A happy picture taken during a visit by King George to Sunderland in 1918.

and his presence was heartily appreciated by the soldiers. How deeply impressed he was by all that he saw was reflected afterwards by the approval he gave to the " Battle of the Somme " films— " the public," he said, " should see the pictures that they may have some idea of what the Army is doing and what it means."

The King had done untold good to the Army by not allowing himself to be dissuaded from taking the risks of the battlefield. With no shadow of disrespect thousands of soldiers were talking of him as " a real sport." His messages at Christmas to the soldiers and sailors spoke of his " grateful thoughts " " for victories gained, for hardships endured, and for your unfailing cheeriness." " The Empire," he added, " confident in you, remains determined to win." In July of the following year the King, accompanied by the Queen, again visited France and Belgium for ten days ; it was the first time for six centuries that the King and Queen of England had been at a seat of war together.

It was at this stage in the War that the King took a step which gave unqualified satisfaction throughout the British Dominions. He abolished all German titles and dignities in the Royal Family and assumed the family name of Windsor. The style of " Royal Highness " was restricted in future to all children of the Sovereign and to his grandchildren in the male line only. The titles of " Prince " and " Princess " were similarly limited.

The opening of 1918 was sombre in events. Towards the end of March, after the first devastating German attack, the King visited the Western Front for the fifth time. His letter written to Sir Douglas Haig after his return bore witness to the fierceness of the battle still raging, the " indomitable courage and unflinching tenacity with which my splendid troops have withstood the supreme effort of the greater part of the enemy's fighting power." He commended, too, the speed with which casualty clearing stations were enabled to carry out their work, and it so happened that his next public document related to the Red Cross, for it was a letter addressed to *The Times* congratulating that journal on the immense total—£10,000,000—which had then been raised for the needs of the Joint War Committee's Fund, and which was afterwards largely exceeded. In May he reviewed a regiment of the United States National Army at Buckingham Palace.

In July the King and Queen celebrated their Silver Wedding. The occasion was purposely shorn of elaborate ceremony, but

N

there was a visit to the City, a special service in St. Paul's, and at Guildhall a presentation to the King by the Lord Mayor, on behalf of the citizens, of a cheque for £53,000, to be devoted to such charities as the King might desire.

At last, on November 11, the fighting was over; and it fell to the King to express without the impending shadow of more slaughter, but happily and finally, the faith which had always been in him from the first day of the War. To the Navy his message went :

Ever since that fateful Fourth of August, 1914, I have remained steadfast in my confidence that, whether fortune frowned or smiled, the Royal Navy would once more prove the sure shield of the British Empire in the hour of trial. . . . I am proud to have served in the Navy, I am prouder still to be its Head on this memorable day.

The King's Address to " all ranks of the Army of the British Empire, Home, Dominion, Colonial, and Indian Troops," contained the following triumphant passage :

You have traversed a long and weary road ; defeat has more than once stared you in the face ; your ranks have been thinned again and again by wounds, sickness, and death ; but your faith has never faltered, your courage has never failed, your hearts have never known defeat.

In congratulating the Air Force he declared that :

Our aircraft have been ever in the forefront of the battle ; pilots and observers have constantly maintained the offensive throughout the ever-changing fortunes of the day, and in the war zones our gallant dead have lain always beyond the enemies' lines or far out to sea.

It is well to recall these utterances, for the King was far more than their mere official mouthpiece. Even if we were so frigid as to attempt to rule out the personality of the Monarch who was speaking, the historic fact would yet remain that no Sovereign upon earth had ever had occasion to address his sailors and soldiers in such a strain before, to congratulate so many men under arms, to speak for so many parts of the globe's surface, to review in mind the conclusion of so gigantic a conflict. The position in which King George V found himself on Armistice Day was without parallel in the records of monarchy.

On the day following Armistice Day the King and Queen attended in State the Service of Thanksgiving at St. Paul's, and a week later the King sent an inspiring message to his people in reply to addresses from both Houses of Parliament. In the Royal Gallery in the Palace of Westminster, amid Lords and Commons and distinguished representatives of the Dominions and of India, he paid warm tributes to the work of the Forces and their commanders, to the contribution of the Dominions and of India, and to the efforts of the Allies. He called for the creation of a better Britain and for the preservation of the spirit of comradeship which had been shown in the years of the War.

After attending naval and military and other celebrations of the peace, the King again went to France. He arrived, with the Prince of Wales and Prince Albert, in Paris on November 28, and it was believed that never had such a vast concourse assembled in the French capital before. The King and the Princes had spent the night at British Headquarters, and were received on their arrival by President Poincaré. The procession that was formed rode through the streets in high triumph, and everything was most happily symbolical of the union of the two nations. On the following day he was received, on an occasion of even greater popular enthusiasm, by the Municipal Council of Paris, and the climax to his official visit to the French came fittingly when he conferred on Marshal Foch the Order of Merit.

From Paris he set out for the Western Front, where he received a glad welcome from the British Armies, visited battlefields which had only recently been won back from the enemy, and entered the long-tried city of Lille. Among the soldiers he moved often in an informal manner on foot, and was everywhere the object of an affectionate following.

Such may be said to be the culmination of the King's war services. But release from his war duties brought the King little respite. In many respects the culminating event of 1919 was Peace Day, which was kept on June 28, and recalled the scenes before Buckingham Palace which had been previously enacted on Armistice Day. Again thousands flocked to the Royal Residence ; a vociferous call from multitudes was readily answered by the King, who with the Queen and their children stepped forward on a balcony, as guns were booming and echoes reverberating, to say in a few words that peace had been signed, that thus ended the greatest war in history ; that he joined with them there in thanking God. For a long time the King remained on the balcony above the joyful uproar; and the scene was renewed later in the evening when, with the searchlights playing overhead and with " For he's a jolly good fellow " in full swing once again among the people, the King stepped forth, saluted, and bade every one " Good night."

But to all the pageantry and entertainment of friendly potentates at this period there was an earnest side, and the many speeches he was called upon to make, often long and always carefully reasoned, showed a style and a grasp of realities which placed them outside the category of conventional Royal oratory.

The King's journey from Balmoral to London in October, 1919, deserves to be recorded, for he and the Queen travelled the whole distance in one day, some 500 miles, by motor-car ; the railway-men were then on strike. His was the principal part during the Armistice Day celebrations of 1920, when he unveiled the Cenotaph and attended the burial of the Unknown Warrior in Westminster Abbey. The true dignity of his bearing was never seen to better advantage than during those moving ceremonies. In the memory of thousands this view of the King will, perhaps, survive all other recollections of him.

The years that followed were full of anxiety and unsettlement at home and abroad, but the Royal duty has been neither so spec-tacular nor so heavily charged with crisis as it was during the opening and middle periods of the reign. Nevertheless the King remained continually active. Among the events to be recorded here are the marriages of His Majesty's only daughter, Princess Mary, in February, 1922, to Viscount Lascelles, who afterwards succeeded his father as Earl of Harewood ; and of his second son, created Duke of York in 1920, in April, 1923, to Lady Elizabeth Bowes-Lyon ; and the death of Queen Alexandra on November 20, 1925, shortly before her 81st birthday.

The same years witnessed important political changes in Ireland and India and one political experiment at home. In Ireland the old controversies were brought if not to final settlement at least to seeming quiet by the establishment of the Irish Free State and the Parliament of Northern Ireland. In India the Chamber of Princes, promised by Royal Proclamation of December, 1920, was inaugurated by the King's representative, the Duke of Connaught.

King George with Queen Mary in the grounds of Craigweil House, Bognor, during his convalescence in the spring of 1929.

At home political changes were swift. The fall of the Coalition made way for a Conservative Government under Mr. Bonar Law, to whom Mr. Baldwin succeeded. A personal drama, in which the King played a leading part, underlay this appointment. By all the custom of the past Lord Curzon was marked out, alike by his experience and by his seniority in the councils of his party, to succeed Mr. Bonar Law ; but it was Mr. Baldwin whom the King summoned to lead the Ministry. The decision, as was revealed in Lord Curzon's biography, was the King's own. The reasons for the King's choice sprang from his knowledge of character and appreciation of national needs.

The new Government did not long endure. A General Election resulted in the establishment for the first time of a purely Labour Administration, with Mr. Ramsay MacDonald as Prime Minister. The Labour Ministry lasted scarcely a year. At the next General Election the Conservatives were given a commanding majority over all parties ; but the precedent was nevertheless, in spite of its short duration, of great significance. In no respect was it more significant than in the proof which it gave of the King's ability to work with and earn the respect and affection of Labour advisers. That he worked easily with them was in keeping with his whole character, and with his ideal of a genuinely national kingship.

The succeeding years were marked by growing industrial unrest, which culminated in the general strike of 1926. The King shared to the full the refusal of his people to take this dark event tragically, and so soon as it was over exercised the full weight of his authority in the direction of securing the pacification of minds and tempers. In a message to the nation on May 12 he appealed for the elimination of bitterness, recalled how steady and how orderly the country had remained under so severe a trial, and urged that the task of making good the mischief done should be undertaken by a united people.

The next great trial to which the King was subjected was of a personal nature. On November 22, 1928, it was announced that he was suffering from a cold with some fever. This illness grew rapidly worse and developed into toxaemia, culminating in a virulent abscess at the base of the lung. During the last week of November and most of December the King was fighting for his life with characteristic courage ; and it was not until February 11, 1929, that he had recovered sufficiently to be moved to Bognor. On

April 23 the King, on St. George's Day, was able to give thanks for his recovery in a message and to foreshadow an appointed day for a public service of thanksgiving, which was duly held on July 7. During his illness the Royal authority was vested in a Commission consisting of the Queen, the Prince of Wales, the Duke of York, the Archbishop of Canterbury, the Lord Chancellor, and the Prime Minister as " Counsellors of State." It was noticeable after that illness that the King's engagements had to be cancelled if the weather were inclement.

The General Election of 1929 resulted in the return of the second Labour Government. The first act of public policy with which the King was personally associated was the opening of the first Round-Table Conference on Indian Constitutional Reform in November, 1930. It was fitting that one who twenty-five years before had declared that " a wider element of sympathy " in the task of governing India would produce " an ever-abundant and genuine response " should open a conference designed to translate generous sentiment into practical propositions ; and in appealing to the Conference to combine justice with progress, the King added from his heart, " For these things I care deeply."

Next year, 1931, brought with it a grave national crisis, with the making of which the King was dramatically associated. Throughout the year the industrial depression had been deepening and spreading through other countries so far relatively immune. During August there developed what amounted to a flight from the pound. The Government, or some members of it, realized that drastic steps to restore confidence were necessary, but proved unable to agree upon a definite programme.

The King, who had been at Balmoral, returned by special train to London on Sunday, August 23. There he at once engaged in consultation with all the party leaders, Mr. Baldwin and Sir Herbert Samuel having been sent for " on the Prime Minister's advice." The result was their agreement to form a National Government, and for this solution of an awkward and dangerous situation the nation had nobody to thank more than the King himself. It must be pointed out that this step involved not the slightest interference with policy by the Crown. The King kept strictly to his constitutional function of suggesting an association of Ministers by whom he could be advised. It is true that later he helped them in an unpleasant and difficult task by reducing the Civil List by £50,000, but that only showed his willingness, as always, to share in everything which affected his people, and did not mark any Royal inspiration of policy.

On Christmas Day, 1932, the King broadcast throughout his Empire the first of his four Christmas broadcasts. The message took only a few minutes to deliver, but there was universal agreement that it could not have reached a higher level ; and the effect produced when every corner of the Empire actually heard the voice of its Sovereign was profound. It is not too much to say that the message itself embodied in its few simple and moving sentences the epitaph which the King would have written for himself :

To arrive at a reasoned tranquillity within our borders ; to regain prosperity without self-seeking ; and to carry with us those whom the burden of past years has disheartened or overborne. My life's aim has been to serve as I might towards those ends.

An important event in 1933 was the meeting of the World Economic Conference in June, and his address to the delegates, partly in English and partly in French, was broadcast all over the world. Unfortunately the Conference failed, on the whole, to grasp the opportunity, which His Majesty declared had now come, " to harness the new consciousness of the interdependence of nations to the service of mankind."

The note of His Majesty's second Christmas broadcast, which was heard all over the Empire and in America, was struck when he said he was " speaking directly to all the members of our world-wide family." In 1934 the King's health had evidently improved, and he was able to attend ceremonies in many parts of the country. Already in that summer people began to bestir themselves in preparation for the Silver Jubilee of His Majesty's Accession in 1935. It was decided that it should be distinctly an Empire family celebration, and when the marriage of the Duke of Kent and Princess Marina of Greece took place in November the occasion was seized upon by the nation with an enthusiasm which gave a foretaste of the more prolonged rejoicings of the following year. Of the other events of the year mention must be made of the launch of the great Cunarder on the Clyde, the name of which was kept secret until the Queen named her the Queen Mary. In his third Christmas broadcast he spoke again of all the peoples of this

Realm and Empire as bound to him and to one another by the spirit of one great family, and in that spirit we should overcome our anxieties, remembering the other members of the family who were suffering from sickness or from the lack of work and hope.

The Silver Jubilee made of 1935 truly an *annus mirabilis*. It was not so much that the King had reigned for so long; it was that he had reigned so well. The nation seemed to realize, more clearly than ever before, how deeply indebted it was to this intensely English monarch, whose plain good sense and devotion to duty had availed to keep the ship of State on an even keel through years often of grave peril and anxiety.

The great day of the Thanksgiving Service on May 6 happily proved an oasis of brilliant sunshine in a rather cold and dismal spring. The scenes in the streets as the processions drove to and from St. Paul's demonstrated once more, but with an added fervour, the almost passionate loyalty of the people. The service itself, with its familiar psalms and hymns and an impressive address by the Archbishop of Canterbury, was worthy of the occasion. Later in the day the King broadcast a message of gratitude to his peoples. Since it was fated that he was to speak into the microphone but once again, it is fitting that that message should be given in full. The King said:

At the close of this memorable day I must speak to my people everywhere. Yet how can I express what is in my heart? As I passed this morning through cheering multitudes to and from St. Paul's Cathedral, as I thought there of all that these twenty-five years have brought to me and to my country and my Empire, how could I fail to be most deeply moved? Words cannot express my thoughts and feelings. I can only say to you, my very dear people, that the Queen and I thank you from the depth of our hearts for all the loyalty and—may I say?—the love with which this day and always you have surrounded us. I dedicate myself anew to your service for the years that may still be given to me.

I look back on the past with thankfulness to God. My people and I have come through great trials and difficulties together. They are not over. In the midst of this day's rejoicing I grieve to think of the numbers of my people who are still without work. We owe to them, and not least to those who are suffering from any

The Service of Thanksgiving in St. Paul's Cathedral during the Silver Jubilee celebrations.

form of disablement, all the sympathy and help that we can give.
I hope that during this Jubilee Year all who can will do their
utmost to find them work and bring them hope.

Other anxieties may be in store. But I am persuaded that with
God's help they may all be overcome, if we meet them with
confidence, courage, and unity. So I look forward to the future
with faith and hope.

It is to the young that the future belongs. I trust that through
the Fund inaugurated by my dear son, the Prince of Wales, to
commemorate this year many of them throughout this country
may be helped in body, mind, and character to become useful
citizens.

To the children I would like to send a special message. Let me
say this to each of them whom my words may reach : The King
is speaking to YOU. I ask you to remember that in days to come
you will be the citizens of a great Empire. As you grow up always
keep this thought before you ; and when the time comes be ready
and proud to give to your country the service of your work, your
mind, and your heart.

I have been greatly touched by all the greetings which have come
to me to-day from my Dominions and Colonies, from India, and
from this Home Country. My heart goes out to all who may be
listening to me now wherever you may be—here at home in town
or village, or in some far-off corner of the Empire, or it may be
on the high seas.

Let me end my words to you with those which Queen Victoria
used after her Diamond Jubilee thirty-eight years ago. No words
could more truly or simply express my own deep feeling now :
" From my heart I thank my beloved people. May God bless
them."

Striking messages were received from heads of States, and news
came of celebrations in every part of the Empire. At home a great
chain of bonfires prepared by Boy Scouts was started by the King,
who, pressing a button at Buckingham Palace, lighted the first
blaze in Hyde Park. The celebrations continued to the end of
July. Not the least interesting were the four processional drives
which the King and Queen took through North, South, East, and
West London. Their Majesties were deeply touched by the

efforts which had been made even in the poorest districts to hang out decorations which showed how deep was the feeling of the inhabitants.

Among the almost countless other celebrations must be mentioned the national thankoffering, King George's Jubilee Trust, started by the Prince of Wales, and the Empire funds for combating cancer in Canada and tuberculosis in South Africa, for mothers and children in Australia, and for four great benevolent institutions in India. Commemorative medals were struck, a special series of stamps was issued, many trees were planted, and the great events of the reign were pictured in books and films. The Royal Warrant Holders' Association presented to the King a complete country house at Burhill, Surrey, for His Majesty to nominate a suitable occupant.

After the strain of the Jubilee the King suffered from bronchial catarrh, and three weeks' rest at Sandringham was prescribed. In September the engagement was announced of the Duke of Gloucester and Lady Alice Scott. Unfortunately the serious illness of the bride's father, the Duke of Buccleuch, who died before the wedding, necessarily altered the arrangements, and the ceremony took place in the Buckingham Palace Chapel instead of in the Abbey. In October the King was presented with another grandson, Prince Edward, the first child of the Duke and Duchess of Kent. But December brought to His Majesty a severe bereavement in the death of his sister, Princess Victoria, to whom he was known to be devotedly attached.

The fourth of the King's Christmas broadcasts, the last which he was to make, was naturally concerned chiefly with the Jubilee. The address is given in full in Chapter I of this volume.

There have been other monarchs round whose names and characters romance or history has woven a more glittering web ; but of George V no man, woman, or child of all the millions whom he ruled and loved so well could ever think a disparaging thought or speak a disparaging word. And this immunity from criticism he won not by lack of character but by the possession of it ; for his qualities of blunt sincerity, of devotion to duty, of determination to do that which he was doing with all his might, will be dear to the hearts of all who were his people wherever the English tongue is spoken and so long as the English name is honoured.

KING ALFRED'S COLLEGE

LIBRARY

Printed and Published by
THE TIMES PUBLISHING COMPANY, LIMITED
PRINTING HOUSE SQUARE, LONDON, E.C.4
ENGLAND